JAMS & CHUTNEYS

JAMS & CHUTNEYS

PRESERVING THE HARVEST

THANE PRINCE

London   New York   Munich
Melbourne   Delhi

Food photography by Jean Cazals

Project Editor Diana Craig
Designer Carole Ash at Project 360
Editor Siobhán O'Connor
Location photographer Steve Lee
Food Stylist Katie Rogers
Props Stylist Sue Rowlands

FOR DORLING KINDERSLEY
Senior Art Editor Susan Downing
Project Editors Anna Davidson and
Laura Nickoll
Managing Editor Dawn Henderson
Managing Art Editor Christine Keilty
Production Editor Ben Marcus
Production Controller Wendy Penn

First published in Great Britain in 2008
by Dorling Kindersley Limited
80 Strand, London WC2R ORL

Penguin Group (UK)

8 10 9 7

A CIP catalogue record for this book is
available from the British Library

ISBN: 978-1-4053-2954-5

Colour reproduction by
Colourscan, Singapore

Printed and bound by
Leo Paper Products Ltd, China

Discover more at
www.dk.com

Contents

Introduction

What is it about making preserves that so entrances me? It isn't my sweet tooth, as my consumption often lags far behind my production levels. Nor is it, with so many wonderful farmers' markets and delicatessens around, all selling jams, jellies, and pickles of every kind, a void on my larder shelf that needs to be filled. I think the answer is that standing in my kitchen stirring a pan of steaming fruit or vegetables, then potting the resulting mixture into jars, is a truly life-enhancing experience. It links me to all those cooks of the past for whom preserving nature's bounty was a necessity, rather than an indulgence. There is also the frisson of pride that one feels when passing a jewel-bright row of home-made jellies on the larder shelf. And there is joy, too, when offering a dish of brilliant red raspberry jam to a friend or handing a jar in to the local fundraiser, in being able to say: "This? I made it myself."

The really good news about making preserves at home is that, while it might at first appear to be a complex, almost black art, it is wonderfully simple once a few basic rules have been understood. Most recipes are well within the reach of the novice cook. For me, the first rule is to ask myself: "Is this truly worth preserving?" Although I like to feel virtuous, I do not wish to have shelf after shelf filled with jars of courgette pickle made – let's be honest – with huge, overblown vegetable marrows. Whether you buy from the farmers' market or harvest from your own vegetable patch or allotment, preserve only the freshest and best of the crop. In the case of chutneys, ketchups, and sauces, there is a little leeway, as here you can use just-overripe tomatoes, plums, etc; for jams, jellies, and pickles, however, only top-drawer will do. Making your own preserves will lend a seasonal quality to your cooking. Beginning with spring's elderflowers, you can traverse the year, potting jars with the first fruits of summer, as well as the last ones of autumn. Even when winter has you in its icy grip, a simmering pan of pickled dried figs or the vibrancy of cranberry vodka can cheer a cook's day.

Another aspect of preserve making that can seem confusing is the terminology. When is a jam not a jam, but a conserve? In this book, I've used the term "jam" when the fruit tends to break down during cooking, "preserve" when there are large chunks of fruit, and "conserve" when the fruits remain whole. This is only a rough guide, and you will no doubt find inconsistencies, as some jams simply cry

out to be called preserves, while occasionally conserve seems to be the name of choice. Pickles, on the other hand, are more clearly defined. A pickle is a vegetable or fruit preserve that is essentially raw, preserved in spiced vinegar. Pickles have nowhere to hide in their clear vinegar-filled jars, so the vegetables used must always be of the first quality, without blemish or bruise. Making chutneys is to my mind one of life's great pleasures. From chopping the onions and grating the ginger to simmering the rich and fragrant mixture, making a large pan of chutney can lift the lowest of spirits. But a word of caution here: don't leave the pan unattended while it simmers, as there is a real tendency for the chutney to catch just at the moment it's ready. Burnt chutney enhances no one's life. Finally, flavouring your own spirits and making your own liqueurs is simplicity itself. Buy good-quality own-brand vodka or gin, and use top-quality fragrant fruits. I store most of these liqueurs in the freezer, where they develop a pleasant consistency, and the cold ameliorates the rather sweet flavour. Serve these home-made liqueurs in your smallest, prettiest glasses – then sit back to enjoy the compliments.

Whether you are new to the kitchen or an experienced cook, I hope you will find here recipes that spark memories of meals eaten when young, some hint of holidays in exotic locations, and new ideas that tempt you into the kitchen, to chop, grate, and slice your way to the perfect preserve.

Thane Prince

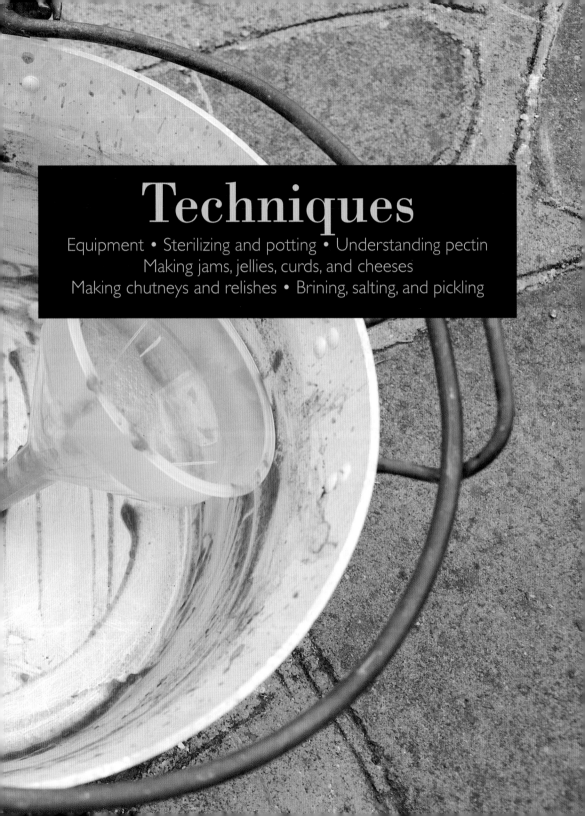

Techniques

Equipment • Sterilizing and potting • Understanding pectin
Making jams, jellies, curds, and cheeses
Making chutneys and relishes • Brining, salting, and pickling

Equipment

Much of the equipment needed to make preserves will probably already be part of your kitchen armoury, but there are a few specialist extras you may require, depending on what you want to make. Check out the preserve-maker's kit that is listed here, and buy or borrow additional equipment as necessary.

Preparing and cooking

PRESERVING PAN

JAM FUNNEL

GRATERS AND SIEVES

SPOONS

PRESERVING PAN

The best pan to use is one that is wider than it is deep. This conducts heat quickly, so that the jam or jelly reduces fast, retaining its fresh flavour, and boils rapidly, which enables it to achieve a set. For chutneys and relishes, it is important that the pan also has a heavy base to achieve an even heat. Go for stainless-steel or enamelled pans, avoiding aluminium, as this reacts with the acids in fruit and with vinegar. Preserving pans are available from kitchen shops and mail-order outlets, or you can improvise. I use an enamelled cast-iron casserole dish 30cm (12in) wide and 15cm (6in) deep.

JELLY BAGS AND STAND

A jelly bag stand and two or three jelly bags (see p18) are a good investment, or improvise by dripping the juice through a fine-woven cloth such as butter muslin or a clean old tea towel, hung between the upended legs of a stool. Wash and scald

bags, muslin, and tea towels before use. When dry, press with a hot iron to sterilize.

MEASURING EQUIPMENT
- Scales for accurate weighing of fruit, vegetables, and sugar.
- 1-litre (1¾-pint) measuring jug and a 500ml (1-pint) measuring jug (optional).
- Spoon measures for accurate weighing of spices, etc.

GRATERS AND SIEVES
- Microplane or similar grater for ginger, garlic, and zest.

- Mouli grater for grating vegetables.
- Sieve to remove pips from jam, if liked.

SPOONS
- Large slotted spoon for removing scum.
- Wooden spoons for stirring and for the flake test (see p17).
- Metal spoons for tasting, etc.

JAM FUNNEL
Try to find a wide-mouthed funnel, as this will make it easier to fill the jars when potting.

Potting

CONTAINERS

Jars must be scrupulously clean and sterilized before use. A dishwasher set on hot fulfils both these requirements, so running the jars through the machine to be ready when the jam is due to be potted is a good idea. Alternatively, wash the jars in hot, soapy water, rinse well, then drain until nearly dry. Put in a cold oven and heat at 150°C (300°F/Gas 2) for 10–15 minutes. Olive oil and vinegar bottles, well washed, dried, and sealed with a lined screwtop or cork lid, are good for flavoured vinegars. Pretty bottles with hinged glass tops and rubber seals, available from hardware outlets and specialist preserving suppliers, are excellent for all vinegars, sauces, and liqueurs.

COVERS

Lids with vinegar-proof inner plastic or rubber rings are the best all-round covers, and there is no need to use waxed paper circles. Lids with no inner rings may be used for vinegar-free preserves, or jars can be sealed with cellophane covers. Dip each cover in water and place, damp side down, over the jar. Stretch the cellophane tightly, holding it in place with a rubber band. In both cases, top the preserve with a waxed paper circle first, cut to fit the top of the jar. Place this directly on the hot preserve, then screw on the lid or stretch over the cellophane cover.

INNER PLASTIC OR RUBBER RINGS must be used to seal chutneys and pickles.

EXISTING LIDS may be used, provided that they show no signs of rust or other deterioration.

CELLOPHANE COVERS, stretched over jars, will tighten as the jam cools.

GLASS CONTAINERS without chips or cracks can be recycled to use for potting preserves.

Potting jams and chutneys

It's worth taking a little time to consider how you will pot your preserves. The size and shape of the jar you use depend on the preserve it will contain. Breakfast marmalade is fine in a large, plain pot, but jellies and pickles to give as gifts will look better in small, interestingly shaped jars. I like to save pretty jars to keep for future use.

How to pot sweet preserves

Once you are happy that your jam or jelly has reached setting point, you need to pot it while the preserve is still hot.

1 GETTING READY
Have ready hot clean sterilized jars, clean sterilized lids (if using), a spotlessly clean jam funnel, and a ladle or large metal spoon. Position the jars on a baking tray or heatproof surface, close to the pan to minimize spills.

2 FILLING THE JARS
Set the funnel over the first jar and ladle the preserve into it, allowing the preserve to fill the jar to within 1cm (½in) of the top. Take care to try not to dribble the preserve round the top of the jar.

3 SEALING THE JARS
If using wax discs (see p11), place these on top of the hot jam at once, then cover with the cellophane jam covers, if using. If you are using lids, place them loosely on the hot jars, and tighten later once the jars are cool.

FILLING THE JARS

SEALING THE JARS

Microwaving jam

Microwave jams are simple and fun. Thinner than those made on a stove, they must be stored in the refrigerator, but are quickly made. The basic principle of microwave jam is to take 500g (1lb 2oz) of prepared fruit and 350g (12oz) sugar, plus the juice of a lemon. Put in a deep glass bowl with a capacity of at least 2 litres (3½ litres). Microwave on High for 2- to 3-minute intervals, stirring often, until the setting point is reached. To test, put a spoonful of jam on a cold plate and allow to cool. When thick enough, pot into sterilized jars, and store in the refrigerator.

How to pot savoury preserves

The only key difference between potting sweet preserves and savoury ones is that the latter require vinegar-proof lids.

1 GETTING READY
Have ready hot sterilized jars with vinegar-proof lids (see p11), a jam funnel, and a ladle or large metal spoon. Place these on a baking tray or heatproof surface near the preserving pan.

2 FILLING THE JARS
Using the jam funnel, spoon the hot preserve into the jars, leaving about 1–2cm (½–¾in) head space. If a chutney or relish is very thick or chunky, it is sometimes necessary to use a spoon to pack the mixture down into the jars to avoid air gaps. I use a clean metal teaspoon to do this.

3 SEALING THE JARS
Once the jar is filled, screw on the lids, or close them in the case of Kilner jars. You may need to tighten screwtop lids again once the jars have cooled, to create a proper seal.

Storing your preserves

• **Labelling** Do be sure to label your jars clearly, both with the name of the preserve and the date when it was potted. I always think I'll remember what is in which jar, but chutneys can look remarkably like jam!
• **Where to store** Unless otherwise stated, store all preserves in a cool, dark cupboard or larder. Once opened, store in the refrigerator and use within the stated time.

Heat processing

The water-bath or heat processing method offers additional protection against contamination by moulds or bacteria. Cellophane-covered jars are not suitable.

• **Filling the pan** You need a specialist water-canner or a large lidded saucepan into which you can fit a rack at the bottom. Put the pan on the hob, and half-fill with boiling water. Set the filled and tightly sealed jars on the rack so that they are close but not touching. Resting on the rack, the jars are protected from the direct heat source beneath. Add more boiling water until the jars are submerged by 2–2.5cm (¾–1in).
• **Boiling the jars** Cover the pan with a lid, bring the water to the boil, and, once boiling, start timing. Process the jars for 10–15 minutes at 85°C (185°F) for sweet preserves and 100°C (212°F) for savoury.
• **Storing the jars** Remove the jars using tongs, and allow to cool before storing in a cool, dark place. For further information, consult the US Department of Agriculture website. Please note this method is for processing preserves only, and not for canning raw fruits and vegetables.

Making sweet preserves

A shelf lined with jams and jellies, brightly coloured and full of promise, is easily within even the most modest cook's grasp. Home-made jam has a freshness that shop-bought alternatives cannot compete with, so get out your largest pan and get cooking.

Ingredients for sweet preserves

FRUIT AND VEGETABLES

Always use best-quality fruit and vegetables – it is pointless preserving anything second-rate. They should be firm, just ripe, and without blemishes. Try to make your preserves as soon as possible after the fruit and vegetables are picked, and make sure everything is clean and grit-free. Hand-picked berries can be sorted and, if very soft (such as raspberries) and dust-free, won't need washing. Strawberries, redcurrants, etc. should be rinsed under cold running water; rinse more robust fruit under warm water. A good scrub in cold water cleans most vegetables that aren't being peeled. To remove the wax coating on bought fruit such as some apples and most citrus, scrub the fruit in hot water with a plastic scourer.

SUGAR

For a good set, you need the correct quantities of sugar, pectin, and acid. White granulated gives as good a result as more expensive preserving sugars. Raw sugar (light and dark muscovado, molasses, Demerara, and golden granulated) can be used, but make the jam darker and can mask the fruit's fresh flavour. An exception is dark full-flavoured marmalade: here, I always opt for raw sugar. When making marmalade with sweet oranges, I use sugar with added pectin. The ratio of sugar to acid and pectin allows a set, so sugar must be carefully weighed. It must also be completely dissolved before the jam or jelly is boiled, so stir over a low heat until no grittiness remains, then increase to a full rolling boil (see p16).

Understanding pectin

• With commercial pectin, the amount needed is in direct ratio to the amount of sugar used. The correct quantity will be marked on the box or bottle, so follow the manufacturer's instructions.

• Make your own pectin by blitzing leftover lemon shells with water. Boil the mixture in a non-reactive saucepan, then allow the juices to drip through a jelly bag (see p208). Use within 2 days.

• Adding fruit that is high in pectin to fruit that lacks enough is another way to achieve a good set in your jam or jelly. Apples, redcurrants, and gooseberries are all pectin-rich.

PECTIN

When combined with sugar and acid, pectin – which is a naturally occurring soluble fibre – forms a bond that causes jam to set. Fruits vary in their pectin content; if a fruit is low in this fibre, it needs to be boiled for a long time to achieve the right concentration of pectin. Adding extra pectin allows for a shorter boiling time and thus a fresher-tasting jam. You can add extra pectin in three ways: with commercial pectin, by making your own (see above), or by adding fruits high in pectin to a jam or jelly being made with fruits that are low in pectin. Commercial pectin is available in liquid or powder form. I have used liquid pectin in this book for convenience, but powdered pectin works equally well.

ACID

Acidity is the final concern when making sweet preserves. This is quite simple: does the fruit taste roughly as acid as lemon juice? For example, gooseberries, raspberries, currants, and cooking apples when boiled all taste very acid. If the fruit does not have that sharp tang, you will need to acidify it further. The simplest way is to add freshly squeezed lemon juice. Juice from other high-acid fruit can also be used, with redcurrant juice being the most common. Powdered citric or tartaric acid is another option: 1 teaspoon powder in 50ml (1¾fl oz) water is the equivalent of 2 tablespoons lemon juice. Adding currant, sour apple, or gooseberry juice can supply both the acid and pectin needed.

How to make jam

Cooking jam involves first cooking the fruit, then boiling the mixture until it reaches setting point. Depending on the fruit used, sugar is added at various stages.

1 COOKING THE FRUIT
Cook the fruit gently, with or without sugar. With delicate fruits, such as raspberries, add the sugar at the start of cooking. For tougher or thicker-skinned fruits, such as blueberries, blackcurrants, cranberries, and citrus, you must boil the fruit or peel first to soften it, then add the sugar and cook until the sugar has dissolved. Add pectin and acid (lemon juice), if using, according to the method.

2 RAPID BOILING
Increase the heat and bring the mixture to a "full rolling boil". You can tell when your jam has reached this point because it will be boiling so hard that you will not be able to stir the bubbles down using a wooden spoon. Boil the mixture hard for the required time, so that the pectin interacts with the sugar to achieve a set.

3 SKIMMING
Skim off any scum as it rises to the surface (see p18). When skimming marmalade, make sure you do so as soon as the mixture begins to boil; otherwise the scum will bond with the peel later, once the jars are cool.

4 TESTING FOR A SET
Study your jam: as it reaches setting point, the mixture will begin to thicken a little around the sides of the pan, will boil more sluggishly, and the bubbles will "plop", rather than froth. I find that the best method is to test once after 3–5 minutes of boiling, then every 2–3 minutes until a set is shown. Always turn off the heat while you test the jam.

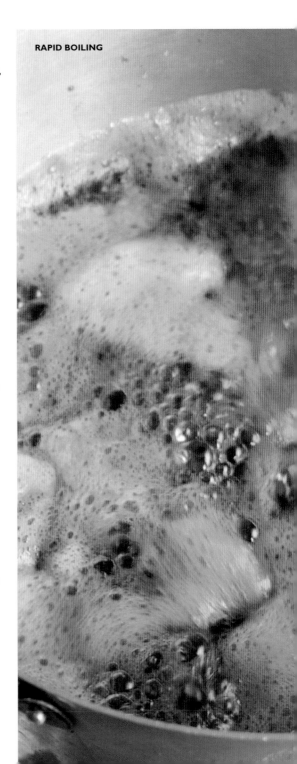

RAPID BOILING

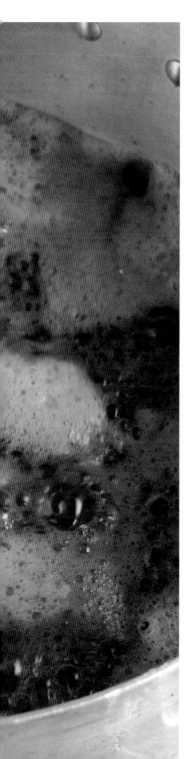

The flake test Using a clean wooden spoon, scoop up a small amount of jam. Allow it to cool for a moment, then gently tilt the spoon to pour the jam back into the pot. If the final part of the jam falls in a flake, rather than a stream, the jam is ready.

The wrinkle test Keep a supply of plates in the refrigerator or freezer. Take a plate, then spoon on about 1 teaspoon of jam. Allow the jam to cool, then push it from the side with your finger. If the surface of the jam wrinkles, it is ready.

How to make jellies

Jellies are made from the strained juice of the fruit, which is cooked first, strained through a jelly bag, and the pulp discarded.

1 COOKING THE FRUIT
Simmer the fruit in water, without any sugar, until it is soft.

2 STRAINING THE FRUIT
Allow the resulting pulp to drip through a scalded jelly bag, piece of muslin, or tea towel for at least 12 hours, to extract all the juice. Do not be tempted to squeeze the bag, as this will cause the jelly to be cloudy.

3 ADDING THE SUGAR
Measure the juice and add the sugar, usually in the ratio of 450g (1lb) sugar to each 600ml (1 pint) liquid, or according to the method.

4 BOILING AND SKIMMING
Bring to a full rolling boil, as for jam (see p16), skimming off any scum. The simplest method is to use a shallow slotted or draining spoon, and a bowl of warm water. Carefully skim the scum from the surface of the mixture, then dip the spoon into the water each time to ensure a clean finish. Take care not to stir the scum down into the mixture. If you are adding flowers, chopped herbs, or seeds, it is best to do so after skimming.

5 TESTING FOR A SET
Test for a set using either the flake test or the wrinkle test (see p17).

STRAINING THE FRUIT

BOILING AND SKIMMING

SIEVING THE MIXTURE

How to make curds, butters, and cheeses

Traditionally, fruit curds always incorporate dairy products and eggs, while fruit butters and fruit cheeses have no dairy products. Fruit cheeses were originally always potted into moulds, then turned out and sliced.

1 SIEVING THE MIXTURE
As the fruit is not usually peeled when making fruit butters and cheeses, the mixture is sieved to remove the peel and pips.

2 TESTING FOR A SET
With fruit curd, cook the mixture without boiling, stirring constantly, until it coats the back of a spoon. The curd will continue to thicken as it cools. To test fruit butter, spread a little on a plate; if no rim of liquid appears around the edge of the mixture, the fruit butter is ready. Test fruit cheese by drawing a spoon across the bottom of the pan: it should leave a clear line through the fruit cheese.

3 POURING INTO A MOULD
If you wish to use your fruit butter or cheese at once, it can be set in a mould when it has reached setting point, then sliced and served.

How to make vinegars, cordials, and drinks

Many fruits and herbs can be used to make vinegars, cordials, and flavoured alcohols. You need to choose good-quality flavourings, so go for ripe fruit, fresh bright herbs, and freshly ground or crushed spices. Vinegars and alcohols, on the other hand, should be of high quality but bland taste. I use white wine vinegar of at least 6 per cent alcohol content for vinegars, and vodka for liqueurs.

POURING INTO A MOULD

Making savoury preserves

Savoury preserves such as chutneys and pickles don't have the immediacy of jams and jellies, as maturing the mix is often necessary for optimum taste. I love making them, all the while thinking of the promise of good things to come lined up in the larder.

Ingredients for savoury preserves

FRUIT AND VEGETABLES

For chutneys, relishes, ketchups, and sauces, you can use slightly overripe and even some less than perfect specimens, as long as you cut out and discard any bruised or damaged parts. Pickles, though, need the best-quality ingredients: they will not be cooked for a long period, if at all, so the freshness of the ingredients must always shine through. As with making jams and jellies, you need to scrub off the wax coating on any bought fruit that has been treated in this way before using it in any of your preserves.

SUGAR

I usually use raw sugar such as muscovado for chutneys, as it gives a wonderfully deep flavour and colour. Fresher-tasting relishes are better made with white granulated or light unrefined sugars such as Demerara. Muscovado sugar is available in three main types: light, dark, and molasses. These types vary according to the amount of raw molasses that is left in the sugar. For most chutneys, light muscovado is best.

Understanding vinegar

• Vinegar is made by adding the Acetobacter bacterium to a spirit, wine, or grain base. This causes the liquid to ferment and eventually oxidize, leading to the production of acetic acid.

• Chutneys, relishes, and similar preserves are quite forgiving in their requirements and can be made with any vinegar without having a detrimental effect on the finished product.

• Pickles are more exacting when it comes to the choice of vinegar. They require a vinegar with an acidity of at least 6 per cent to ensure that they are preserved properly and hence keep well.

VINEGAR

• **Red and white wine vinegars** are usually 6 per cent acid and are suitable for all pickle- and chutney-making. They have a good, clean flavour.

• **Cider vinegar** has an acidity of about 5 per cent. It has a soft, smooth taste and is an excellent choice for chutneys and similar preserves, but it is not acid enough for pickles.

• **Malt vinegars** usually have an acidity of 6 per cent, making them suitable for all forms of chutney- and pickle-making. Malt vinegars have a distinct flavour; distilled malt vinegar is flavourless.

• **Rice wine vinegar** is a soft-tasting vinegar and tends to have an acidity of only 5 per cent. Pickles made with it will not have a long shelf life and should be stored in the refrigerator.

SPICES

To ensure that they are at their most potent, dry spices should always be ground just before you need them. Few of us would relish a cup of coffee made from beans ground several months, let alone years, ago, but that is just what we often do when we need spices. Any flavouring that relies on volatile oils for its taste needs to be used as soon as possible after the oils have been released. I use a dedicated coffee grinder to grind spices, but a good result can be obtained using a mortar and pestle, plus a bit of hard work.

How to make chutneys and relishes

The excess water in fruit and vegetables must be driven off or it spoils the finished preserve. In chutneys and relishes, this is achieved by long, slow boiling, which also gives a good mounding consistency. Sugar and vinegar are the preserving elements.

1 PREPARING THE INGREDIENTS
Chop the vegetables to an even size: 1cm (½in) cubes are about right. Larger dried fruit, such as dates and peaches, are also best chopped before use. Finely grate ginger and garlic. Use a Microplane or similar grater to zest citrus fruit; when juicing the fruit, sieve to remove any pips. Grind all whole spices using a coffee grinder or a mortar and pestle.

2 COOKING THE MIXTURE
Put all the ingredients in the preserving pan, and simmer over a low heat, stirring often to ensure that the sugar dissolves. Increase the heat to medium, and simmer the preserve until thick – this can take an hour or more. It is important to stir the mixture from time to time, especially towards the end of cooking, when it can catch on the bottom of the pan.

3 TESTING
To test whether the preserve is ready, drag a wooden spoon through the mixture on the bottom of the pan. The spoon should leave a clear channel, with perhaps a little liquid seeping back. If the mixture flows back to cover the channel, boil for a little longer.

4 REDUCING TO A PURÉE
For ketchups and sauces, there is an additional step, which involves reducing the cooked mixture to a purée. This is done by whizzing it in a blender, passing it through a mouli, or pushing it through a fine sieve.

COOKING THE MIXTURE

TESTING

COVERING WITH
VINEGAR

How to make pickles and vinegars

In pickles, salt is used to drive off the water in the vegetables that would otherwise dilute the vinegar used and hence spoil the final product. This is done either by brining or by dry-salting. Salt also seasons the pickles and contributes to the preserving process.

1 BRINING OR DRY-SALTING

Whether you brine or dry-salt the ingredients depends on the vegetables being used. Those with a high water content, such as cucumbers, cabbage, courgettes, and aubergines, are best dry-salted rather than brined.

Brining To make a typical brining solution, dissolve 225g (8oz) table salt in 1.5 litres (2¾ pints) water in a large glass, china, or plastic bowl. Immerse the prepared vegetables, and

leave to soak for 12–24 hours. Drain, rinse well under cold running water, and spread out on clean tea towels to dry. Brine should always be used cold to avoid encouraging bacterial growth.

Dry-salting In a large glass, china, or plastic bowl, arrange the prepared vegetables in layers, sprinkling each layer with salt. Leave to soak overnight, then drain the vegetables, rinse under cold running water, and spread out on clean tea towels to dry.

2 COVERING WITH VINEGAR

Hot pickles are those that are cooked for only a short time, often as little as 2–3 minutes, while cold pickles generally have hot vinegar poured over the cold packed vegetables. With hot pickles, the vegetables are brined, cooked for a short time to ensure the vegetables stay crisp, then potted in spiced vinegar. Cold pickles, on the other hand, are brined, then simply covered with spiced vinegar without prior cooking.

Summer berries

Blackberries • Blackcurrants • Blueberries • Cranberries
Cherries • Gooseberries • Grapes • Loganberries
Raspberries • Strawberries

Picking berries from a late summer garden can yield a surprising number of varieties that provide the essential ingredients for pots of deliciously dark-hued jumbleberry jam – perfect for spreading on freshly made crusty bread.

Jumbleberry jam

⏱ TAKES 20 MINUTES   🍯 MAKES 750G (1LB 10OZ)   🫙 KEEPS FOR UP TO 1 YEAR

1   In a preserving pan, mix together the berries and sugar, then stir in the lemon juice. Warm the mixture over a low heat, stirring gently, until the sugar dissolves.

2   Increase the heat and bring to the boil. Cook at a full rolling boil for 3–5 minutes until the jam reaches setting point.

3   Pot into hot sterilized jars, seal, and label.

INGREDIENTS

450g (1lb) mixed berries (raspberries, redcurrants, blackcurrants, etc.)

450g (1lb) white granulated sugar

freshly squeezed juice of 1 large lemon

CHOOSING BERRIES

One of the great advantages of this recipe is that it doesn't matter precisely what proportions of different berries you use. It is the total weight that matters, and this must equal the weight of the sugar. If using strawberries, they will need to be hulled first, and currants will need to be destemmed.

Sue Laing, a good friend of mine who lives on a fruit farm in Norfolk, is justly famous for her jams. To achieve the right cooking heat, make separate batches rather than doubling quantities.

Sue's strawberry preserve

 TAKES 25 MINUTES   MAKES 1.8KG (4LB)   KEEPS FOR 6–9 MONTHS

1   In a large china or glass bowl, layer the strawberries and sugar, then sprinkle with the juice. Cover with cling film and leave for 24 hours.

2   Scrape the contents of the bowl into a preserving pan, and bring slowly to the boil. Allow the mixture to bubble over a low heat for 5 minutes, then remove from the heat, cover, and allow to stand for 48 hours.

3   Return the pan to the heat, and bring the mixture back to the boil. Skim thoroughly. Boil until a setting point has been reached. The jam will always be quite soft, so I boil it until it thickens to my liking.

4   Remove from the heat, pot into hot sterilized jars, seal, and label.

INGREDIENTS

1.5kg (3lb 3oz) small, freshly picked strawberries

1.5kg (3lb 3oz) white granulated sugar

freshly squeezed juice of 4 lemons

I like to make jam with cultivated blackberries and jelly with wild ones. The latter have masses of pips that I think are better removed, as they can be rather intrusive in the finished preserve.

Blackberry jam

 TAKES 15 MINUTES   MAKES 1.8KG (4LB)   KEEPS FOR UP TO 1 YEAR

1   Wash the berries, then drain them well, spreading them out on a tea towel to ensure as much water as possible is absorbed. Alternatively, leave to drain in a large sieve or colander.

2   Put in a large preserving pan with the lemon juice and sugar. Warm over a gentle heat, stirring gently from time to time, until the sugar has dissolved and the berries have softened and released their juice.

3   Cook at a full rolling boil for 3 minutes. Stir in the pectin and boil for a further 2 minutes, then test for a set.

4   Once the jam has reached setting point, pot into hot sterilized jars, seal, and label.

INGREDIENTS

1kg (2¼lb) blackberries

freshly squeezed juice of 1 lemon

1 kg (2¼lb) white granulated sugar

125g (4oz) liquid pectin

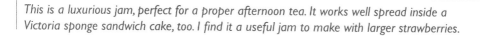

This is a luxurious jam, perfect for a proper afternoon tea. It works well spread inside a Victoria sponge sandwich cake, too. I find it a useful jam to make with larger strawberries.

Strawberry, rhubarb, and vanilla jam

🕐 TAKES 20 MINUTES   🥘 MAKES 1.25KG (2¼LB)   🗄 KEEPS FOR UP TO 1 YEAR

1   Cut the rhubarb into 2.5cm (1in) lengths, then cut the strawberries into slices about 0.5cm (¼in) thick.

2   In a large china or glass bowl, layer the fruit with the sugar. Pour over the lemon juice and leave in a cool place overnight.

3   Scrape the fruit, sugar, and all the juice into a preserving pan, and warm over a low heat. Stir from time to time, then bring the mixture to a full rolling boil. Cook for 2 minutes, then turn off the heat and stir in the pectin.

4   Return the mixture to the boil, and boil for a further 2 minutes or until the jam has reached setting point. Remove from the heat, skim off any scum from the top of the jam, and stir in the vanilla seeds.

5   Allow to cool for 5 minutes before potting into hot sterilized jars, sealing, and labelling.

VARIATION
For a spicier jam, replace the vanilla seeds with 60g (2oz) fresh root ginger, peeled and finely grated.

INGREDIENTS

1.25kg (2¼lb) rhubarb

600g (1lb 5oz) strawberries

1.8kg (4lb) white granulated sugar

freshly squeezed juice of 2 lemons

250g (9oz) liquid pectin

seeds scraped from 1 large vanilla pod

Preserving summer berries

CHOOSING FRUITS FOR A GOOD SET

Ripe, headily scented berries are what summer is all about. Pick-your-own farms, farm stalls, and farmers' markets allow us access to quantities of beautifully ripe fruit, and it is this that you need for making the best and most flavourful preserves. As the right balance of acid and pectin is necessary to obtain a set, slightly underripe berries or those just on the point of ripeness, which contain the highest levels of both, are the best choice. Pick your berries on a dry day.

High pectin

• **Black, white, and red currants** are high in both acid and pectin. They can be combined with other fruit to help facilitate a set. Make sure you remove all the stems.
• **Gooseberries** can be used fully ripe, as they are high in both acid and pectin. The juice can be used to add pectin to soft-setting jams such as strawberry. Some varieties of green gooseberry produce pink jam.
• **Cranberries** usually contain sufficient pectin to make both jams and jellies, without the need for extra to be added. Look for dry and unshrivelled bright red berries, and store in the refrigerator until needed.

Moderate pectin

• **Raspberries** have moderate amounts of acid and pectin, and are highly scented and flavoured. Choose uncrushed whole, ripe berries. Use soon after harvest, as they are fragile and ferment easily.
• **Loganberries, tayberries, and boysenberries** are a cross between blackberries and raspberries. They contain moderate amounts of acid and pectin. Used with raspberries, they will give both a deeper colour and more pronounced flavour.

CURRANTS of all colours are pectin- and acid-rich.

RASPBERRIES are among the most popular berries for preserving and need some added pectin to aid setting.

Low pectin

- **Strawberries** are low in both acid and pectin. Look for small, firm, slightly underripe berries.
- **Blueberries** contain little acid or pectin, and are best used for preserves when fully ripe.
- **Blackberries**, if cultivated, contain more acid than their wild cousins. Avoid berries that are dusty. Late-season berries contain less acid and pectin, so add apples for a good set.

BLUEBERRIES AND STRAWBERRIES require added pectin for a set.

Loganberries are a hybrid berry made by crossing raspberries with blackberries. They have a tarter flavour than raspberries and, like blackberries, tend to retain a white inner core. This makes them more time-consuming to prepare, as the cores must be removed before cooking.

Loganberry jam

🕐 TAKES 20 MINUTES   🥄 MAKES 1.35KG (3LB)   🫙 KEEPS FOR UP TO 1 YEAR

1 Remove the white cores from the berries. Put the berries and sugar in a preserving pan, and cook over a low heat until the sugar dissolves and the fruit softens.

2 Bring to the boil and boil rapidly for 5–7 minutes until the jam has just reached setting point.

3 Pot into hot sterilized jars, seal, and label. If you prefer a pip-free jam, sieve before potting.

INGREDIENTS

750g (1lb 10oz) loganberries

750g (1lb 10oz) white granulated sugar

Gooseberries have both a high acid and a high pectin content, so this tart jam sets quickly and is one of the easiest to make. The colour will vary, depending on the variety and ripeness of the berries. The tartness of this delicious jam makes it a perfect foil for scones and cream.

Gooseberry jam

 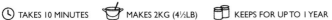

🕐 TAKES 10 MINUTES   🥄 MAKES 2KG (4½LB)   🫙 KEEPS FOR UP TO 1 YEAR

1 Top and tail the gooseberries (this does take some time, but improves the finished jam). Wash the berries, shake off any excess water, and put in a large preserving pan with 120ml (4fl oz) water.

2 Cover and bring to the boil. Reduce the heat, and simmer for about 5 minutes until the berries are very soft.

3 Remove the lid and stir in the sugar. When the sugar has dissolved, increase the heat and boil rapidly for about 2 minutes until the jam has reached setting point.

4 Pot into hot sterilized jars, seal, and label.

INGREDIENTS

1kg (2¼lb) gooseberries

1.25kg (2¾lb) white granulated sugar

It's important to cook currants well before adding the sugar or they will become as tough as little bullets. Once this has been done, and the sugar added, reaching setting point will not take long. Blackcurrants should be as fresh as possible – the older they are, the tougher the skins.

Blackcurrant jam

🕐 TAKES 30–40 MINUTES   🥘 MAKES 2KG (4½LB)   🥫 KEEPS FOR UP TO 1 YEAR

1   Wash the currants well to remove any dust and grit. Drain and put in a preserving pan with 1 litre (1¾ pints) water.

2   Bring to the boil, cover, and simmer the mixture over a low heat for about 20 minutes until the fruit is very soft.

3   Add the sugar, stirring gently until dissolved. Increase the heat and boil rapidly for about 15 minutes until the jam reaches setting point.

4   Pot into hot sterilized jars, seal, and label.

INGREDIENTS

1kg (2¼lb) blackcurrants

1.35kg (3lb) white granulated sugar

Cranberries are often overlooked as a teatime preserve, being more often considered an accompaniment to roast turkey. This tangy jam redresses the balance, and has a good colour and flavour. Enjoy it with hot buttered toast, crumpets, or English muffins, eaten by the fireside.

Cranberry and orange preserve

🕐 TAKES 25 MINUTES   🥘 MAKES 650G (1LB 7OZ)   🥫 KEEPS FOR UP TO 1 YEAR

1   Put the cranberries and orange juice in a large preserving pan, cover, and cook over a moderate heat for about 15 minutes until the fruit is very soft.

2   Stir in the sugar and zest, and cook over a low heat until the sugar has dissolved. Increase the heat and cook at a full rolling boil for 3–5 minutes until the preserve reaches setting point.

3   Pot into hot sterilized jars, seal, and label.

INGREDIENTS

500g (1lb 2oz) fresh cranberries

freshly squeezed juice of 3 oranges

500g (1lb 2oz) white granulated sugar

grated zest of 2 oranges

This is probably my favourite recipe for jam. It reminds me of summer days, the heady scent of fruit at the pick-your-own farm, and traditional English teas of jam, scones, and cream in the garden. I always make small batches, as this jam is best eaten fresh. Don't look for a firm set – the best raspberry jam should always be a little runny.

Best-ever raspberry jam

🕐 TAKES 15–20 MINUTES   🍲 MAKES 900G (2LB)   🥫 KEEPS FOR UP TO 1 YEAR

1   Put the berries and sugar in a preserving pan. Simmer over a low heat, stirring occasionally, until the fruit has softened and the sugar has dissolved.

2   Bring to boiling point and boil rapidly for 5–7 minutes until the mixture reaches setting point.

3   Pot into hot sterilized jars, seal, and label.

VARIATION

In winter, when snow is abundant, evoke the scent of summer by making this jam with frozen raspberries instead of fresh ones.

INGREDIENTS

450g (1lb) freshly picked raspberries

450g (1lb) white granulated sugar

RETAINING THE PIPS

Some folks worry about the pips in this jam. If you are one of them, by all means sieve out the pips while the jam is hot. Be warned, though, that in doing so you will reduce the weight – and also, I believe, the flavour – of the jam. After all, you would not discard the pips in fresh raspberries …

Lemon curd is a well-known, perennial favourite, but curds can be made with a wide variety of fruit. I love raspberry curd. Use it to fill roulades and sponges, or fold it into lightly whipped cream and pipe into meringues for an irresistible treat.

Raspberry curd

 TAKES 30–40 MINUTES   MAKES 1.6KG (3½LB)   KEEPS FOR ABOUT 3 MONTHS

1 Put the berries and 2 tablespoons water in a large saucepan, and bring to boiling point. Simmer, covered, for 5 minutes or until the fruit is very soft.

2 Rub the mixture through a sieve into the top half of a large double boiler. You can also cook this curd in a heatproof bowl over a pan of simmering water if you don't have a double boiler.

3 Add the sugar, butter, and eggs. Place over the lowest possible heat and, using a balloon whisk, gently whisk the mixture until the sugar has dissolved and the butter has melted.

4 Continue to simmer, stirring constantly with a wooden spoon, until the mixture thickens, then turn off the heat and stir again. If you feel that the curd isn't quite thick enough, heat again, but remember that it will thicken further as it cools.

5 When the curd has reached the desired consistency, pot into hot sterilized jars, and label. Store in the refrigerator.

INGREDIENTS

1kg (2¼lb) raspberries

450g (1lb) white granulated sugar

115g (4oz) salted butter, diced

4 large eggs, beaten

EXTRA EQUIPMENT

double boiler (optional)

PREVENTING CURDLING

Stir with a wooden spoon and keep the mixture moving while you cook to ensure it does not stick to the pan. On no account must it boil or it may curdle. At the first sign of bubbles, remove from the heat immediately, set the top half of the pan (or heatproof bowl) in a large bowl of iced water, and stir the curd with the wooden spoon. The curd has reached the right consistency when it coats the back of the spoon.

Although this preserve does require you to pit the cherries – which is a messy job – its wonderful taste and scent make it worth the extra bother. To ease the task, invite a friend around to chat to you while you work. Making this jam is a wonderful way to use up a glut of berries from heavily cropping summer trees.

Black cherry preserve

 TAKES 30 MINUTES  MAKES 1.35KG (3LB)   KEEPS FOR UP TO 1 YEAR

1 If using fresh cherries, remove any stalks and pit the fruits, using gloves to protect your hands from staining.

2 Put the cherries and 150ml (5fl oz) water in a large preserving pan, and bring to the boil. Cover and simmer for about 15 minutes until the cherries are tender. Turn off the heat and add the sugar and lemon juice, stirring until the sugar dissolves.

3 Return the mixture to the boil, and boil for 2 minutes, stirring occasionally and skimming off any scum that rises to the surface. Turn off the heat again, add the pectin, and stir in well.

4 Cook at a full rolling boil for a further 8–10 minutes, then test for a set. Once the jam has reached setting point, pot into hot sterilized jars, seal, and label.

VARIATION
For those who do not have the time – or the inclination – to pit the fruit, frozen cherries come ready-pitted and work well in this recipe.

INGREDIENTS

1kg (2¼lb) cherries

1kg (2¼lb) white granulated sugar

freshly squeezed juice of 2 lemons

250g (9oz) liquid pectin

I have a small Morello cherry tree in my garden, so I make a few pots of this delicious jam each year. Morello cherries are wonderfully coloured but quite small, which means that pitting them is a labour of love. Enhance plain yogurt with a generous swirl of this jam, or use it as a topping for hot buttered crumpets or scones at teatime on crisp winter Sundays.

Morello cherry jam

🕐 TAKES 10 MINUTES   🥄 MAKES 1.35KG (3LB)   🥫 KEEPS FOR UP TO 1 YEAR

1 Begin by pitting the cherries, using gloves to prevent your hands becoming stained.

2 Put the cherries, sugar, and lemon juice in a preserving pan, and simmer over a low heat, stirring to dissolve the sugar. Bring the mixture to the boil, then reduce the heat and simmer for 5 minutes or until the cherries are cooked.

3 Stir in the pectin. Boil for 2 minutes before turning off the heat and testing for a set.

4 When the jam has reached setting point, pot into hot sterilized jars, seal, and label.

VARIATION
For an altogether more wicked preserve, add 75ml (2½fl oz) kirsch to the jam once setting point has been reached, and stir in well. The jam will be a little softer, but delicious.

INGREDIENTS

1kg (2¼lb) Morello cherries

750g (1lb 10oz) white granulated sugar

freshly squeezed juice of 2 lemons

125g (4½oz) liquid pectin

To prevent them becoming tough and chewy, blueberries should always be well cooked before the sugar is added. As they are low in acid and pectin, you need to add both these ingredients for a successful preserve. Blueberry jam goes well with American-style pancakes, or it may be swirled into plain yogurt or used as a filling for a layer cake.

Blueberry preserve

 TAKES 30 MINUTES   MAKES 1.6KG (3LB)   KEEPS FOR UP TO 1 YEAR

1   Put the blueberries in a preserving pan with 150ml (5fl oz) water and the lemon juice. Bring the mixture to the boil, then reduce the heat, cover, and simmer for 10 minutes or until the fruit is soft.

2   Add the sugar, stirring over a low heat until the sugar has dissolved. Increase the heat and boil rapidly for 3–4 minutes.

3   Add the pectin and boil for a further minute before turning off the heat and testing for a set.

4   When the jam has reached setting point, pot into hot sterilized jars, seal, and label.

VARIATION
Wild blueberries work well in this recipe. Being smaller than cultivated blueberries does not mean wild ones need less cooking time, though – they must be boiled until soft before you add the sugar.

INGREDIENTS

1kg (2¼lb) blueberries

freshly squeezed juice of 4 lemons

1kg (2¼lb) white granulated sugar

115g (4oz) liquid pectin

Traditionally used in peanut butter and jelly sandwiches, grape jelly is best made with very fresh, slightly underripe grapes – perfect if you have a prolific vine in your greenhouse.

Grape jelly

 TAKES 25 MINUTES  MAKES 800G (1¾LB) KEEPS FOR UP TO 1 YEAR

1 Put the grapes – which can be a mixture of red and white – in a stainless-steel saucepan and crush them: I use a potato masher. Add 150ml (5fl oz) water, then bring to the boil, reduce the heat, cover, and simmer for 10–15 minutes until the grapes are very soft.

2 Crush the grapes again, then spoon the mixture into a jelly bag and allow to drip for 12 hours.

3 Measure the juice, then measure out the correct amount of sugar, pectin, and lemon juice. Put the juice and sugar in a preserving pan, and bring slowly to the boil, stirring until the sugar has dissolved.

4 Add the pectin, increase the heat, and boil rapidly for 3–5 minutes until the jelly has set. Pot into hot sterilized jars, seal, and label.

INGREDIENTS

1kg (2¼lb) grapes

FOR EVERY 500ML (16FL OZ) JUICE

675g (1½lb) caster sugar

100g (3½oz) liquid pectin

freshly squeezed juice of 1 large lemon

Use a relatively inexpensive port and either well-scrubbed or unwaxed fruit for this good all-round jelly. For a more savoury version, stir in 1 tablespoon chopped rosemary with the zests.

Port wine and orange jelly

 TAKES 15 MINUTES  MAKES 1.6KG (3½LB) KEEPS FOR UP TO 1 YEAR

1 Put the port, orange and lemon juice, and sugar in a large preserving pan, and bring the mixture slowly to the boil.

2 Once the sugar has dissolved, bring to a full rolling boil and cook for 10–15 minutes. Add the pectin and boil for a further 2 minutes, skimming off any scum from the top of the jelly.

3 Turn off the heat and test for a set. If the jelly has reached setting point, stir in the orange and lemon zest. Boil for 30 seconds.

4 Turn off the heat allow the jelly to stand for 3–4 minutes to cool slightly, then pot into hot sterilized jars, seal, and label.

INGREDIENTS

750ml (1¼ pints) red port

grated zest and juice of 3 large oranges

grated zest and juice of 1 lemon

1kg (2¼lb) white granulated sugar

250g (9oz) liquid pectin

This recipes makes a delicious clear preserve. Made with Shiraz wine, the result will be a beautiful amber-coloured jelly to partner scones or cold meats.

Shiraz wine jelly

 TAKES 20 MINUTES    MAKES 1KG (2¼LB)   KEEPS FOR UP TO 1 YEAR

1 In a preserving pan, mix the wine with the lemon juice and pectin. Bring to the boil, whisking from time to time to ensure that all the ingredients are thoroughly combined.

2 Add the sugar and stir the mixture over a low heat until the sugar has dissolved completely.

3 Increase the heat and bring the mixture to a full rolling boil, using a slotted spoon to skim off any scum that rises to the surface during cooking. Boil for 2 minutes, then turn off the heat and test for a set.

4 If the jelly has not set, return the mixture to the boil and cook at a full rolling boil for a further minute, then test for a set again.

5 When the jelly has reached setting point, pot into small hot sterilized jars, seal, and label.

VARIATION
Any full-bodied wine can be used to make this preserve. Try Chardonnay or port instead of Shiraz.

INGREDIENTS

750ml (1¼ pints) Shiraz wine

freshly squeezed juice of 2 large lemons

250g (9oz) liquid pectin

900g (2lb) white granulated sugar

The astringent flavour and bright red skins of cranberries add both acid and colour to jams, jellies, relishes, and ketchups. This jelly is the classic accompaniment to those Thanksgiving and Christmas turkey meals. Easy to make and pretty to look at, it is the perfect seasonal gift.

Cranberry jelly

 TAKES 45 MINUTES    MAKES 800G (1¾LB)   KEEPS FOR UP TO 1 YEAR

1   Put the berries and 1 litre (1¾ pints) water in a stainless-steel saucepan and bring to the boil, then reduce the heat and simmer, covered, for 25–30 minutes until the fruit is very soft.

2   Mash the mixture well – I find a potato masher does a good job – then spoon into a jelly bag and allow to drip overnight.

3   Measure the resulting liquid: you should have about 750ml (1¼ pints). If you have more, boil rapidly to reduce to this quantity; if less, add water to make up to the correct quantity.

4   Pour the liquid into a preserving pan and add the sugar. Warm over a low heat until the sugar dissolves, then increase the heat and cook at a full rolling boil for about 15 minutes. Test for a set.

5   Once the jelly has reached setting point, skim off any scum from the top, then pot the jelly into hot sterilized jars, seal, and label.

INGREDIENTS

450g (1lb) cranberries

500g (1lb 2oz) white granulated sugar

VARIATION
The grated zest and juice of 2 sweet oranges can be added to the fruit before cooking – or try a 10cm (4in) cinnamon stick, lightly crushed.

This scrumptious jelly has all the flavour of raspberry jam, but none of the pips. Simple to produce, and easily made with frozen berries, it needs neither acid nor pectin.

Raspberry jelly

 TAKES 20 MINUTES  MAKES 1KG (2¼LB) KEEPS FOR UP TO 1 YEAR

1 Put the berries and 300ml (10fl oz) water in a stainless-steel saucepan and bring to the boil. Reduce the heat and simmer for 10–15 minutes until the berries are soft. Spoon into a jelly bag and allow to drip overnight.

2 Measure the juice, then measure the sugar in the correct proportion. For 750ml (1¼ pints) juice, you will need 750g (1lb 10oz) sugar. Pour the juice into a clean preserving pan and stir in the sugar.

3 Warm the mixture over a low heat until the sugar has dissolved, then increase the heat and boil rapidly for about 5 minutes. Skim off any scum from the jelly as it rises to the surface.

4 Turn off the heat and test for a set. When the jam has reached setting point, pot into hot sterilized jars, seal, and label.

INGREDIENTS

1kg (2¼lb) raspberries, thawed if frozen

100g (3½oz) white granulated sugar for every 100ml (3½fl oz) juice

High in pectin and acid, and so needing only added sugar for a good set, redcurrants make a delightful preserve for both sweet and savoury dishes. Try blackcurrants or white currants, too.

Redcurrant jelly

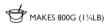 TAKES 40 MINUTES  MAKES 800G (1¾LB) KEEPS FOR UP TO 1 YEAR

1 Put the fruit and 500ml (16fl oz) water in a stainless-steel pan. Bring to the boil, cover, and simmer for 30 minutes or until the fruit is soft.

2 Mash lightly – a potato masher is ideal for this – then spoon into a jelly bag and allow the mixture to drip for 12 hours or overnight.

3 Measure the resulting juice and the appropriate quantity of sugar. Put both in a clean preserving pan. Stir over a low heat until the sugar has dissolved, then boil rapidly until setting point has been reached.

4 Pot into hot sterilized jars, seal, and label.

INGREDIENTS

1kg (2¼lb) redcurrants

500g (1lb 2oz) white granulated sugar for every 500ml (16fl oz) juice

Fruit vinegars not only taste good, but are also wonderfully coloured and make a refreshing change from balsamic. Slightly sweet, they go well with goat's cheese salads and fish dishes.

Berry vinegar

 TAKES 5 MINUTES   MAKES 500ML (16FL OZ)   KEEPS FOR 3–6 MONTHS

1   Put the berries and sugar in a saucepan and heat gently, stirring occasionally, until the juices run and the sugar has dissolved.

2   Transfer the mixture to a glass jug or bowl, and stir in the vinegar. Cover with cling film and leave to infuse for at least 1 week, but preferably 3 weeks.

3   Strain the vinegar into a clean bottle and use for dressings.

INGREDIENTS

250g (9oz) blackberries, raspberries or blackcurrants, thawed if frozen

60g (2oz) caster sugar

400ml (14fl oz) white wine vinegar

I make this lovely drink each December to serve, ice cold, in tiny liqueur glasses after lunch or dinner. The colour is wonderfully festive and the cranberries are rich in vitamin C, making this almost a drink that is good for you! Don't forget to save the original vodka bottle and its screwtop lid, as you will need them for storing the drink after the initial infusing.

Frozen cranberry vodka

 TAKES 5 MINUTES   MAKES 750ML (1¼ PINTS)    KEEPS FOR 1 YEAR, FROZEN

1   Put the cranberries and sugar in the goblet of a food processor or blender, and whiz until the berries are finely chopped.

2   Transfer the mixture to a glass or china bowl, and pour over the vodka. Stir and cover with a double layer of cling film. Leave the bowl in a cool, dark place for 3–4 weeks.

3   Strain the mixture through muslin and pour it into the saved vodka bottle. Screw on the lid and store in the freezer until needed.

INGREDIENTS

450g (1lb) cranberries

225g (8oz) white granulated sugar

750ml (1¼ pints) vodka

Home-made drinks that mimic French cordials are simple to put together. I make this fruity gin as well as cassis, raspberry vodka, and both blackberry and cranberry vodka (see p47). Use supermarket-brand spirits and really fresh, ripe fruit. Pour the drinks back into the original bottles and, when ready, serve either as liqueurs or diluted with white wine.

Raspberry gin

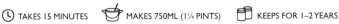 TAKES 15 MINUTES   MAKES 750ML (1¼ PINTS)   KEEPS FOR 1–2 YEARS

1 Put the raspberries and sugar in a stainless-steel saucepan and heat gently, stirring occasionally, until the fruit juices begin to run and the sugar has dissolved.

2 Transfer the mixture to a glass bowl or jug, and pour over the gin. Stir, then cover with cling film, sealing tightly.

3 Stir daily for 4 or 5 days, then strain into the original bottles, seal, and store in a cupboard or dark larder, or in the freezer. Taste after about 8 weeks, adding more sugar if you think it necessary. The gin is ready to drink after about 3 months, but is best left for 1 year. Add a few fresh raspberries to each glass when serving, if liked.

VARIATION
For blackberry vodka, replace the raspberries with blackberries and the gin with vodka. Store in the freezer after making.

INGREDIENTS

450g (1lb) raspberries, plus extra to serve (optional)

225g (8oz) white granulated sugar

600ml (1 pint) gin

Stone fruit

Apricots • Damsons • Greengages • Mirabelles
Nectarines • Peaches
Plums • Prunes

This is a wonderfully fragrant jam, vying with raspberry as my very favourite — perfect on hot buttered toast, spooned onto scones, or as a luscious and slightly tart filling for sponge cakes. Be sure to use apricots that are ripe but only just so.

Apricot jam

🕐 TAKES 25 MINUTES   🍲 MAKES 1.25KG (2¾LB)   📦 KEEPS FOR 9 MONTHS

1 Cut the apricots into quarters and remove the stones. Put the fruit, 400ml (14fl oz) water, and lemon juice in a preserving pan, and bring the mixture to the boil. Simmer over a low heat, stirring occasionally, for about 15 minutes until the fruit is very soft.

2 Add the sugar, allowing it to dissolve into the fruit. Try not to stir the mixture too much, as this will break up the apricots — you want to retain some large chunks to give the jam texture.

3 Increase the heat and bring the mixture to a full rolling boil. Boil for 4–5 minutes, then stir in the pectin and boil for a further 2 minutes. If making the jam without pectin, it will need to be cooked at a full rolling boil for 15 minutes: this will produce a softish jam.

4 Remove from the heat and test for a set.

5 When the jam has reached setting point, pot it into hot sterilized jars, seal, and label.

INGREDIENTS

1kg (2¼lb) just-ripe apricots

freshly squeezed juice of 3 lemons

1kg (2¼lb) white granulated sugar

125g (4½oz) liquid pectin (optional)

CHOOSING FRUIT

I prefer to look for larger apricots when making this preserve, as I find them better for jam making than smaller, sweeter ones. To make the most of the finished jam, choose fruit that is fragrant, just-ripe, and blemish-free.

This jam is very simple to make because you do not need to test for a set. Based on dried apricots, all it requires is simmering until thick. Lime juice and zest add the necessary tartness. Make this preserve when fresh fruit is hard to come by to bring cheer to dark winter days.

Apricot and lime jam

🕐 TAKES 30 MINUTES   🍲 MAKES 500G (1LB 2OZ)   🗄 KEEPS FOR 1 YEAR

1   Ready-to-eat dried apricots require no pre-soaking, so you can use them straight from the packet. Wash the apricots, then chop roughly and transfer to a preserving pan. Add 600ml (1 pint) water and the lime zest and juice. Bring to the boil, reduce the heat, and simmer the mixture for 10–15 minutes until the apricots are tender.

2   Now add the sugar, stirring over a low heat until it has dissolved.

3   Increase the heat to medium, and continue to simmer for about 15 minutes depending on the size of the pan, stirring occasionally, until the jam is thick.

4   Pot into hot sterilized jars, seal, and label.

VARIATION
Dried peaches or dried pears could replace the apricots in this recipe. If using dried ready-to-eat pears, I like to chop in some sugared crystallized ginger, too, for extra zing.

INGREDIENTS

225g (8oz) ready-to-eat dried apricots

finely grated zest and freshly squeezed juice of 1 lime

225g (8oz) white granulated sugar

Fruit cheeses are really concentrated fruit purées, spiced and cooked until firm enough to slice. They are delicious with both meat and cheese. This recipe is ideal for damsons, as it allows the small fruits to be cooked whole, then rubbed through a sieve to remove skin and pips.

Damson cheese

TAKES 1½ HOURS   MAKES 1KG (2¼LB)   KEEPS FOR 1 YEAR

1 Put the damsons and 1 litre (1¾ pints) water in a large preserving pan. Using a mallet or rolling pin, give the ginger a good bash, then add this to the pot. Bring the mixture to the boil, then reduce the heat and simmer for 30 minutes or until the fruit is very soft.

2 Allow the fruit to cool a little, then sieve to remove the stones, skins, and remains of the ginger.

3 Pour the resulting purée into the cleaned preserving pan, and add the sugar. Place the pan over a low heat, and stir frequently until the sugar has dissolved.

4 Increase the heat to medium and allow the mixture to cook for 30–45 minutes until reduced and very thick. You will need to watch carefully towards the end of cooking, as the fruit can catch and burn.

5 To test if the cheese is cooked, scoop out a spoonful, put it on a cold plate, and allow it to cool. It should stay in a mound rather than spread out over the plate. Always remember to turn the heat off while you test jam for a set.

6 When the cheese has reached setting point, pot into hot sterilized jars, seal, and label.

INGREDIENTS

2kg (4½lb) damsons

10cm (4in) piece of fresh root ginger

1.5kg (3lb 3oz) white granulated sugar

Plums are packed full of pectin, so jams made with them set easily. Choosing a variety isn't a problem for this recipe, but larger plums are easier to prepare. Cinnamon is a spice that works especially well with plums. For a stylish touch, add a piece of cinnamon stick to each pot.

Red plum and cinnamon jam

🕐 TAKES 20 MINUTES   🍲 MAKES 1.25KG (2¾LB)   🗄 KEEPS FOR UP TO 1 YEAR

1   Cut the plums into halves or quarters, depending on size. Remove the stones and discard them.

2   Put the prepared fruit in a preserving pan, and add 250ml (8fl oz) water, sugar, and cinnamon. Cook gently over a moderate heat for 10–15 minutes, stirring, until the sugar has dissolved.

3   Now increase the heat, bring to a full rolling boil, and cook for 3–5 minutes until the jam has reached setting point.

4   Pot into hot sterilized jars, adding a cinnamon stick to each one, if you like. Seal and label.

INGREDIENTS

1kg (2¼lb) red plums

1kg (2¼lb) white granulated sugar

10cm (4in) cinnamon stick, finely ground, plus extra cinnamon sticks for potting (optional)

WATCHING FOR A SET

As plums contain a high quantity of pectin, watch carefully for a set – cook for a few minutes too long and the jam will be very thick and stiff. This jam is made with red plums, which is my family's preference, but yellow plum jam tastes good, too.

Preserving with plums

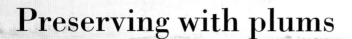

VICTORIA

VARIETY OF USES

There are literally thousands of varieties of plums, and every one has its place in the making of preserves, jams, or chutneys. Plums can be the base for fruit sauces and ketchups, can add bulk to chutneys, and were always the base fruit of school "red jam". High in pectin and acid, they set easily and so are a dream fruit for novice jam-makers.

What to look for

For jams and preserves, choose firm, just-ripe plums with a bloom on the skin and no blemishes. For sauces, ketchups, and jellies, you can use overripe or slightly less perfect plums, as long as you cut away all the bruises. Always avoid any fruit that has mould on, it as this will taint the preserve. Plum jam tends to be quite plain in flavour, so try adding spices to enhance the taste. Cinnamon works well, as do vanilla, five-spice powder, and star anise.

GREENGAGE

PREPARATION AND USES

Plums may be divided into three main categories:
Small plums, such as damsons, mirabelles, and sloes, are better suited to jelly-making because stoning them is time-consuming.
Larger plums, such as Victoria, Santa Rosa, and President, are best cut into quarters before cooking.
Greengages are in a category of their own. They make the most delicious of plum jams and need no additional spicing.

FORTUNE RED

MIRABELLES

DAMSONS

PRESIDENT

GOLDEN PLUM

SANTA ROSA

In France, greengages are known by the wonderful name Reine Claude. They are smaller than many plums, but make a scrumptious preserve. I like to use slightly less sugar than usual with this fruit to preserve as much of the fresh taste as possible. While the skin and flesh of the ripe fruit are a delightful yellowish-green, cooking can change the colour of the finished jam.

Greengage jam

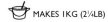 TAKES 15–20 MINUTES  MAKES 1KG (2¼LB) KEEPS FOR 6 MONTHS

1 Cut the greengages into quarters, removing and discarding all the stones.

2 Put the fruit and 200ml (7fl oz) water in a preserving pan. Place the pan over a low heat and gently cook the mixture for 10 minutes, stirring from time to time, until the greengages begin to give up some of their juice and start to soften.

3 Add the sugar and continue to simmer, stirring, until all the sugar has dissolved.

4 Increase the heat, bring the mixture to a full rolling boil, and cook rapidly for about 5 minutes, skimming off any scum that rises to the surface. Test for a set.

5 Once the jam has reached setting point, pot into hot sterilized jars, seal, and label.

INGREDIENTS

1kg (2¼lb) greengages

750g (1lb 10oz) white granulated sugar

Nuts add an interesting texture to this delightful summer preserve. I store all my nuts in the freezer to ensure that they stay as fresh as possible. Let them thaw completely before chopping them. Potted into pretty jars and tied with ribbons, this preserve makes a lovely gift.

Peach and pistachio preserve

 TAKES 20 MINUTES   MAKES 1.25KG (2¾LB)   KEEPS FOR 6–9 MONTHS

1 First, peel the peaches. Bring a large saucepan of water to the boil. Meanwhile, cut a cross in the base of each peach. When the water is boiling, drop in the fruit, turn off the heat, and leave for 3–4 minutes. Lift one peach from the water and see if the skin slips off easily. If it does, drain the remaining peaches. If not, return the peach to the water and wait for a further 2–3 minutes before draining all the fruit and peeling it.

2 Chop the peach flesh into 1cm (½in) dice, discarding the stones.

3 Put the flesh, sugar, and lemon juice in a preserving pan, and bring the mixture slowly to the boil. Cook at a full rolling boil for 4–5 minutes, skimming off any scum that rises to the surface.

4 Stir in the chopped nuts and the pectin, and simmer for 1 minute before testing for a set.

5 Once the preserve has reached setting point, pot into hot sterilized jars, seal, and label.

INGREDIENTS

1kg (2¼lb) ripe peaches

800g (1¾lb) white granulated sugar

freshly squeezed juice of 2 lemons

60g (2oz) pistachio nuts, chopped

125g (4½oz) liquid pectin

"Sugaring" the nectarines overnight draws out the juice, which dissolves the sugar. This sugary liquid is then boiled down first, so that the fruit is cooked for less time and stays more chunky.

Nectarine conserve

🕐 TAKES 15 MINUTES   🍲 MAKES 1.6KG (3½LB)   📦 KEEPS FOR 6–9 MONTHS

1   Cut the nectarines into 1cm (½in) cubes. In a large, clean glass or china bowl, arrange in alternate layers with the sugar, continuing until all the fruit and sugar have been used. Pour over the lemon juice, cover with a cloth, and leave overnight.

2   Carefully lift the fruit from the sugary liquid using a slotted spoon, or drain in a sieve. Reserve the liquid and set the fruit aside.

3   Scrape all the liquid and any undissolved sugar into a preserving pan. Heat slowly, stirring, until the sugar has dissolved. Boil rapidly for 5 minutes, then add the fruit and cook for a further 5 minutes.

4   Add the pectin and cook at a full rolling boil for 2 minutes or until setting point is reached. Pot into hot sterilized jars, seal, and label.

INGREDIENTS

1kg (2¼lb) ripe nectarines

1kg (2¼lb) white granulated sugar

freshly squeezed juice of 2 lemons

125g (4½oz) liquid pectin

There is no need to skin the peaches for this lovely pink jelly. Redcurrants replace added pectin and acid, making for a freshly flavoured preserve.

Peach and redcurrant jelly

🕐 TAKES 25 MINUTES   🍲 MAKES 1.5KG (3LB 3OZ)   📦 KEEPS FOR 6–9 MONTHS

1   Cut the peaches into 1cm (1½in) dice, discarding the stones. Put in a large preserving pan with the currants and 500ml (16fl oz) water. Bring to the boil, then simmer for about 20 minutes until very soft.

2   Spoon the mixture into a jelly bag positioned over a clean bowl and allow to drip overnight. Put the juice in the cleaned preserving pan: you should have about 750ml (1¼ pints). Add the sugar. Stir over a low heat until the sugar has dissolved.

3   Increase the heat and cook at a full rolling boil for 3–5 minutes until setting point is reached. Pot into hot sterilized jars, seal, and label.

INGREDIENTS

1kg (2½lb) ripe peaches

400g (14oz) redcurrants, stalks removed

750g (1lb 10oz) white granulated sugar

Tiny yellow plums with a distinctive flavour, mirabelles are more suited to jelly-making than to jams, as stoning them is time-consuming work. This preserve has a lovely colour and sets well.

Mirabelle jelly

⏱ TAKES 30 MINUTES　🍲 MAKES 1.25KG (2¾LB)　🥫 KEEPS FOR 6–9 MONTHS

INGREDIENTS

1kg (2¼lb) mirabelle plums

90g (3oz) white granulated sugar for every 100ml (3½fl oz) mirabelle juice

freshly squeezed juice of 2 lemons

1　Put the mirabelles and 500ml (16fl oz) water in a saucepan, and simmer for 15–20 minutes until the fruit is very soft.

2　Spoon the mixture into a jelly bag, and allow to drip overnight.

3　Measure the resulting juice: you will have about 600ml (1 pint). Weigh out the correct amount of sugar. Pour the mirabelle juice into a preserving pan, and add the lemon juice and sugar.

4　Bring the mixture slowly to the boil, then simmer for 2–3 minutes until the sugar dissolves, stirring frequently. Now cook it at a full rolling boil for 2–3 minutes, skimming off any scum. Test for a set.

5　Once the jelly has reached setting point, pot into hot sterilized jars, seal, and label.

I use either "no-soak" or "ready-to-eat" prunes for this recipe. They are wonderful spooned over ice cream, eaten for a special breakfast with Greek-style yogurt, or baked in rich almond cakes.

Prunes in brandy

⏱ TAKES 25 MINUTES　🍲 MAKES 500G (1LB 2OZ)　🥫 KEEPS FOR 2 YEARS

INGREDIENTS

1 tsp Earl Grey or other tea leaves

500g (1lb 2oz) no-soak or ready-to-eat prunes

4–6 tbsp light raw muscovado sugar

400ml (14fl oz) brandy, plus extra to cover if required

1　Using the leaves of your choice, make 1 litre (1¾ pints) of tea. Strain the brewed tea into a bowl and add the prunes, ensuring that they are all covered. Leave to soak overnight.

2　Drain the prunes well, patting them dry with kitchen paper.

3　Pack the prunes into 2 × 250g (9oz) jars, adding 2–3 tablespoons sugar to each jar and pouring in sufficient brandy to cover the fruit.

4　Seal, label, and store. The prunes will be ready to consume in 3–4 months. Both the prunes and the brandy can be used.

This dual-purpose recipe comes from my summer holidays in central France. The peaches make a heady topping for ice cream and the brandy on its own is a delicious sticky after-dinner liqueur. For a simple but enticing dessert, whisk some of the flavoured brandy into cream, add the chopped fruit and some crumbled meringue, then spoon into wine goblets.

Peaches in brandy

 NO COOKING   MAKES 2 LITRES (3½ PINTS)   KEEPS FOR 6–9 MONTHS

1   Cut a small cross in the base of each peach, then put them in a deep bowl. Cover the fruit with boiling water and allow them to sit for 2 minutes. Remove a peach from the water and try to peel the skin. If the skin comes away easily, drain and peel all of the fruit. If not, leave for another minute.

2   Cut the peaches into quarters and arrange in layers in the jar, alternating with layers of sugar. Push the vanilla pod down one side of the jar, bending it in half if necessary.

3   Pour over the brandy, then seal and label the jar, shaking it gently to help the sugar start to dissolve.

4   Leave the jar in a cool, dark place for about 3 months, shaking gently about once a week. I serve the brandy straight from the jar, but you can strain it into a clean bottle if you prefer.

INGREDIENTS

3 or 4 large, ripe, unblemished peaches

100g (3½oz) caster sugar

1 vanilla pod, split lengthways

500ml (16fl oz) brandy

EXTRA EQUIPMENT

2-litre (3½-pint) wide-necked glass jar

VARIATION
If preferred, nectarines make a suitable and perhaps slightly more unusual replacement for peaches in this recipe.

Choose slightly unripe peaches for this recipe and, for ease of preparation, ensure that they are not the clingstone variety. Serve this delicious chutney with curries and cheese sandwiches.

Peach and ginger chutney

⏱ TAKES 40 MINUTES   🍲 MAKES 2–2.5KG (4½–5½LB)   📦 KEEPS FOR UP TO 1 YEAR

1 Immerse the peaches in boiling water, then peel (see Peach and pistachio preserve, p62). Chop the flesh, discarding the stones. Chop the onions. Crush the garlic and chillies, and grate the ginger.

2 Put the peach flesh, onion, garlic, and dried fruit in a preserving pan. Stir in the ginger, chilli, and cider vinegar, then stir in the sugar.

3 Bring slowly to the boil over a low heat, stirring occasionally. Once the sugar has dissolved, increase the heat and allow the chutney to bubble for 30–40 minutes until thick, stirring often and ensuring that the chutney at the bottom of the pan does not catch and burn.

4 Pot the chutney into jars, cover with vinegar-proof seals, and label.

INGREDIENTS

1.5kg (3lb 3oz) peaches

2 large onions

6 garlic cloves

3 small dried red chillies

5cm (2in) piece fresh root ginger

500g (1lb 2oz) mixed dried fruit

1 litre (1¾ pints) cider vinegar

675g (1½lb) light muscovado sugar

This softish relish goes well with grilled tuna, chicken kebabs, and hot dogs.

Nectarine and sweetcorn relish

⏱ TAKES 45 MINUTES   🍲 MAKES 1KG (2¼LB)   📦 KEEPS FOR 3 MONTHS

1 Cut the nectarines into 1cm (½in) cubes, discarding the stones. Chop the onions and chillies. Put all the ingredients except the sugar and salt in a large preserving pan, stir well, and bring to the boil. Cover and simmer for 10 minutes. Stir in the sugar and simmer for a further 3–4 minutes until dissolved.

2 Increase the heat to medium and cook the relish for 20–30 minutes until most of the liquid has evaporated. Test to see whether the relish is ready (see p22). Stir in the salt.

3 Pot the relish into hot sterilized jars, cover with vinegar-proof seals, and label. Use within 3 months.

INGREDIENTS

600g (1lb 5oz) nectarines

300g (10oz) red onions

30–60g (1–2oz) red chillies

300g (10oz) sweetcorn kernels

3 garlic cloves, crushed

400ml (14fl oz) white wine vinegar

1 tbsp fresh thyme leaves

200g (7oz) golden granulated sugar

2 tsp salt

A mix of fresh and dried apricots provides the basis for this spicy orange-coloured relish. Serve it with chicken curries, chunks of bread and cheese, and in sandwiches.

Apricot and red onion relish

🕐 TAKES 50 MINUTES   🍲 MAKES 2KG (4½LB)   🥫 KEEPS FOR 1 YEAR

1 Put all the spices in a spice mill, and whiz until the mixture is finely ground. Alternatively, grind the spices using a mortar and pestle, sifting out any large pieces.

2 Put the garlic and ginger in a blender or food processor, and whiz to make a paste, or grind together with the mortar and pestle.

3 Put all the ingredients, including the ground spices and garlic-ginger paste, in a large preserving pan. Stir until thoroughly mixed. Simmer for 10 minutes, stirring occasionally, until the sugar has dissolved.

4 Increase the heat to medium and continue to simmer the relish for 40 minutes or until it is thick and the fruit is cooked, stirring occasionally. Do keep an eye on the mixture towards the end of cooking, as it has a tendency to stick. The relish is ready when a wooden spoon dragged across the bottom of the pan leaves a clear channel in the mixture.

5 Pot the relish into hot sterilized jars, cover with vinegar-proof seals, and label. Store in a cool, dark place.

VARIATION
Any stone fruit works well in this recipe. Perhaps for ease I would choose nectarines as a substitute for apricots, as their thin skins make preparation of this relish a simple process.

INGREDIENTS

2 dried red chillies

2 dried bay leaves

2 tsp coriander seeds

1 tsp allspice berries

1 tsp black peppercorns

1 tsp yellow mustard seeds

cloves from 1 whole head of garlic

10cm (4in) piece of fresh root ginger

1kg (2¼lb) fresh apricots, stoned and chopped

500g (1lb 2oz) ready-to-eat dried apricots, chopped

750g (1lb 10oz) red onions, chopped

200g (7oz) celery, chopped

1 red pepper, deseeded and chopped

1 tbsp salt

750ml (1¼ pints) white wine vinegar

500g (1lb 2oz) Demerara or golden granulated sugar

This plum sauce is most often served with crispy duck, but it could also add a zing to many stir-fries. Away from the Chinese kitchen, I like to serve it with cold meats and cheeses. I also use it as a baste for pork joints or chops towards the end of cooking, to give them extra flavour. Plums of any colour may be used, making this recipe handy if you have a glut of fruit.

Chinese plum sauce

⏱ TAKES 1½ HOURS   🍲 MAKES 1 LITRE (1¾ PINTS)   🫙 KEEPS FOR 1 YEAR

1 Cut the plums in half and remove the stones: this will make sieving easier later on. Put all the ingredients except the sugar and star anise in a large preserving pan. Bring to the boil, cover, and simmer for 20 minutes or until all the ingredients are very soft.

2 Pass the mixture through a mouli or coarse sieve, and return to the cleaned pan.

3 Add the sugar and star anise, and bring back to the boil, stirring frequently to ensure that the sugar dissolves. Simmer the mixture for 30–60 minutes until the sauce is thick and creamy.

4 Pot the plum sauce into hot sterilized bottles, seal with vinegar-proof lids, and label.

VARIATION

If you would like a more fiery sauce, add 4–6 red chillies, deseeded if preferred, then chopped, with the vegetables at the start of cooking.

INGREDIENTS

2kg (4½lb) ripe plums

750g (1lb 10oz) white onions, chopped

cloves from 1–2 whole heads of garlic, chopped

20cm (8in) piece of fresh root ginger, about 400g (14oz), peeled and chopped

250ml light soy sauce

1 litre (1¾ pints) rice wine vinegar

1kg (2¼lb) light muscovado sugar

6 star anise, finely ground

Ketchup doesn't need to be made with tomatoes – I always make mine with plums, a sort of upmarket brown sauce. Full of flavour and sublimely spicy, this ketchup simply demands plump pork sausages and a mound of mashed potato or, better yet, egg and chips.

Spicy plum ketchup

🕐 TAKES 1–1¼ HOURS   🍲 MAKES 1 LITRE (1¾ PINTS)   🥫 KEEPS FOR 12–18 MONTHS

1   Halve and stone the plums, and chop if large. Put in a large preserving pan with the dates, raisins, onion, garlic, and ginger. Add the coriander, allspice, cayenne, and 500ml (16fl oz) of vinegar.

2   Bring the mixture to the boil, then simmer for 30–40 minutes until the fruit is very soft.

3   Allow the mixture to cool, then rub through a mouli or sieve.

4   Return the purée to the cleaned pan. Add the remaining vinegar, turmeric, nutmeg, sugar, and salt. Bring the mixture to the boil. Simmer for 30–45 minutes until reduced to a thick, pouring consistency, stirring frequently.

5   Allow the ketchup to cool, then transfer to hot sterilized jars or bottles, cover with vinegar-proof seals, and label. Store in a cool, dark place or larder for at least a month before use.

VARIATION

If you have a favourite combination of spices, why not experiment here? I sometimes add some celery seed. Dark muscovado sugar, instead of the light variety listed, adds a deeper flavour and one that is more suitable for adult tastes.

INGREDIENTS

2kg (4½lb) plums

175g (6oz) stoned dates, chopped

115g (4oz) raisins

1 large onion, chopped

4 plump garlic cloves, chopped

5cm (2in) piece of fresh root ginger, about 60g (2oz), grated

1 tbsp freshly ground coriander seeds

1 tsp freshly ground allspice berries

good pinch of cayenne pepper

1 litre (1¾ pints) malt or wine vinegar

1 tbsp ground turmeric

½ nutmeg, grated

300g (10oz) light muscovado sugar

60g (2oz) salt, or to taste

This is a lovely fresh-flavoured chutney that has a distinctly oriental feel. I like to use my chillies whole, seeds and all, for a marked fiery finish, but do deseed them if you want a more mellow relish. Good with cheese, I also like to serve this with pork chops, roast pork, and game pie.

Red plum, lime, and coriander chutney

⏱ TAKES 1 HOUR   🍲 MAKES 2KG (4½LB)   🥫 KEEPS FOR 1 YEAR

1   In a spice mill or using a mortar and pestle, grind the cinnamon, coriander, and peppercorns together until you have a fine powder. Halve and stone the plums, then roughly chop.

2   Put all the ingredients in a large preserving pan, and bring slowly to the boil, stirring often to dissolve the sugar.

3   Once the sugar has dissolved, simmer gently for 50–60 minutes until the chutney is thick. Stir frequently towards the end of cooking to prevent the mixture sticking to the bottom of the pan and burning.

4   Once the chutney has reduced and thickened, turn off the heat and allow it to cool for 10 minutes.

5   Pot into hot sterilized jars, cover with vinegar-proof seals, and label. Store in a cool, dark place for at least 1 month before use.

VARIATION
Star anise is a possible spice here, but, as it can be a bit overwhelming, 1 or 2 stars, finely crushed, will suffice.

INGREDIENTS

15cm (6in) cinnamon stick

2 tbsp coriander seeds

1 tsp black peppercorns

2kg (4½lb) red plums

2 large onions, chopped

5 garlic cloves, chopped

2 red chillies, deseeded for a milder flavour, if liked, and chopped

5cm (2in) piece of fresh root ginger, about 60g (2oz), grated

finely grated zest and freshly squeezed juice of 2 limes

finely grated zest and freshly squeezed juice of 1 lemon

500ml (16fl oz) red wine vinegar

500g (1lb 2oz) Demerara or light muscovado sugar

Summer vegetables

Aubergines • Beetroot • Cabbage • Carrots • Cauliflower
Courgettes • Marrow • Mushrooms • Onions • Pumpkin
Rhubarb • Tomatoes

With its affinity for sugar and spices, pumpkin lends itself to both savoury and sweet treatments. Eating this flame-coloured pumpkin butter is akin to tasting autumn. Spread it on buttered toast, eat it on gingerbread, or spoon it onto waffles and serve with whipped cream.

Spiced pumpkin butter

🕐 TAKES 1½ HOURS   🍲 MAKES 1.6KG (1½LB)   📦 KEEPS FOR 6 MONTHS

INGREDIENTS

1 Put the pumpkin in a steamer and steam for 10 minutes or until soft. Transfer to a blender or food processor, and whiz until you have a smooth purée.

2 Transfer the purée to a preserving pan and add the sugar.

3 Using a coffee mill, grind the spices to a fine powder. Alternatively, grind using a mortar and pestle. Stir into the pumpkin purée along with the lemon juice and zest.

4 Simmer the butter over a low heat for 60–90 minutes until very thick, stirring frequently. Take care, as the butter can start spitting as it cooks. The mixture is quite thick to begin with, but needs long cooking to condense and form the butter.

5 When the purée is as thick as it can be (it will begin to catch no matter how often you stir) and when a wooden spoon drawn across the bottom of the pan leaves a clear channel, it is ready for potting. Pot it into hot sterilized jars, seal, and label.

INGREDIENTS

2kg (4½lb) pumpkin, peeled, deseeded, and cut into 2cm (¾in) cubes

600g (1lb 5oz) unrefined sugar

1 cinnamon stick

½ nutmeg

6 cloves

2 mace blades

finely grated zest and freshly squeezed juice of 2 lemons

COOKING IN A STEAMER

Pumpkin has a high water content, so steaming this fruit rather than boiling it in water prevents the pumpkin disintegrating into a mush, preserves more of its vitamin content, and retains more of its flavour. For even cooking, cut into even-sized cubes.

This is a really old-fashioned jam, once made by our mothers and grandmothers. It is still worth thinking about if you have a large ripe marrow left at the end of the summer. Fresh ginger adds the necessary edge to an otherwise subtle flavour.

Marrow and ginger jam

TAKES 25 MINUTES   MAKES 1KG (2¼LB)   KEEPS FOR 6 MONTHS

1   Layer the marrow in a large china or glass bowl, sprinkling each layer with sugar and lemon juice, until all the sugar and juice has been used. Set aside for 24 hours.

2   The next day, drain the liquid from the marrow. Transfer the liquid to a preserving pan, along with any remaining undissolved sugar.

3   Add the lemon zest and ginger to the pan, and bring the mixture to the boil. Boil rapidly for about 20 minutes until the liquid is reduced by roughly half.

4   Add the marrow cubes, and simmer for a further 4–5 minutes until the marrow is soft. Skim off any scum from the surface of the jam.

5   Add the pectin and cook at a full rolling boil for 2 minutes, then test for a set.

6   Once the jam has reached setting point, allow it to stand for up to 20 minutes or until the marrow pieces have settled, then pot into hot sterilized jars, seal, and label.

INGREDIENTS

1.5kg (3lb 3oz) marrow flesh, peeled, deseeded, and cut into 2cm (¾in) cubes

1kg (2¼lb) white granulated sugar

finely grated zest and freshly squeezed juice of 3 lemons, about 120ml (4fl oz)

115g (4oz) fresh root ginger, peeled and grated

250g (9oz) liquid pectin

Quite tooth-achingly sour, rhubarb has a wonderful taste that comes alive with the addition of sugar. While it contains much acid, rhubarb has little pectin, so you will need to add this to achieve a set. Given rhubarb's high acidity, avoid aluminium saucepans in making this recipe.

Rhubarb marmalade

 TAKES 20 MINUTES  MAKES 1.35KG (3LB) KEEPS FOR 6 MONTHS

1 Put the rhubarb, sugar, juice, and zest into a stainless-steel or enamel preserving pan. Bring the mixture slowly to the boil, then simmer over a low heat for 5–8 minutes until the rhubarb is soft and the sugar has dissolved.

2 Now add the pectin and mix in gently, stirring until well combined. Return the marmalade to the boil, and cook for a further 2 minutes before testing for a set.

3 Once the marmalade has reached setting point, pot into hot sterilized jars, seal, and label.

INGREDIENTS

1kg (2¼lb) rhubarb, washed and cut into 1cm (½in) lengths

800g (1¾lb) white granulated sugar

finely grated zest and freshly squeezed juice of 2 oranges

125g (4½oz) liquid pectin

VARIATION
Rhubarb has a particular affinity with ginger, so try adding a little grated fresh root ginger to this recipe to give it a spicy lift.

Carrot makes a bold-coloured jam and spicing it with cardamom seeds adds an exotic feel to this preserve. To find the seeds, split open the green pods and discard them: the seeds lay tucked inside. Serve this spicy jam with wholemeal toast and Cheddar cheese.

Carrot and cardamom jam

🕐 TAKES 25 MINUTES   🍲 MAKES 1.5KG (3LB)   🫙 KEEPS FOR 1 YEAR

1   Put the carrots in a saucepan, cover with water, and boil for 10–15 minutes until tender. Drain the carrots and chop them finely.

2   Put the carrots, lemon, orange zests and juices, and cardamom seeds in a preserving pan. Add the sugar, and cook over a low heat until the sugar has dissolved.

3   Increase the heat and boil the mixture for 5 minutes.

4   Add the pectin, return the mixture to the boil, and cook for a further 2 minutes. Test for a set.

5   Once the jam has reached setting point, leave to cool for a further 10 minutes, then stir to distribute the carrot and cardamom. Pot into hot sterilized jars, seal, and label.

VARIATION

Very young parsnips, cores removed, also have the necessary sweetness to make a tasty and unusual jam. They should be used as soon as possible after purchase to ensure the best possible finished preserve.

INGREDIENTS

500g (1lb 2oz) fresh young carrots, peeled, and cut into 2cm (¾in) lengths

finely grated zest of 2 lemons

freshly squeezed juice of 3 lemons

finely grated zest and freshly squeezed juice of 1 large orange

1 tbsp cardamom seeds

1kg (2¼lb) white granulated sugar

125g (4½oz) liquid pectin

This chutney reminds me of warm Mediterranean sunshine and summer holidays. Aubergine and orange work well together. I use fresh-tasting green chillies in this recipe, but fiery red ones could replace them. Serve with grilled lamb kebabs, and meat or fish tagines.

Aubergine, orange, and coriander chutney

🕐 TAKES I HOUR   🍲 MAKES I.7KG (3¾LB)   🫙 KEEPS FOR UP TO I YEAR

1   Put the spices in a grinder and whiz together until coarsely ground. Alternatively, grind with a mortar and pestle.

2   Put the ground spices and the remaining ingredients in a preserving pan. Cook over a low heat, stirring occasionally, to dissolve the sugar.

3   Once the sugar has dissolved, increase the heat and bring the mixture to the boil. Simmer for I hour, stirring occasionally, until the chutney is very thick. Keep an eye on the mixture as it cooks, because this particular chutney has a tendency to stick and burn.

4   When the mixture has reached the desired consistency – you should be able to make a clear channel with a wooden spoon across the bottom of the pan – pot the chutney into hot sterilized jars, cover with vinegar-proof seals, and label. Store in a cool, dark place.

VARIATION
You can vary the spices used here to suit your taste – fennel seeds work well, as does freshly grated root ginger.

INGREDIENTS

2 tbsp coriander seeds

I tbsp cumin seeds

½ tsp black peppercorns

Ikg (2¼lb) aubergines, trimmed and cut into Icm (½in) dice

600g (Ilb 2oz) red onions, chopped

4 fresh green chillies, deseeded if liked, and chopped

4–6 plump garlic cloves, crushed

finely grated zest and freshly squeezed juice of 2 large oranges

600ml (I pint) cider vinegar

400g (14oz) Demerara sugar

I tbsp salt

Courgettes might not be the first vegetables that come to mind when thinking of chutney-making, but a glut of these flavourful cucurbits is just what's needed to make this tangy pickle, spiced with ginger, mustard, and coriander. I like to serve it with sausage and mash.

Chunky courgette chutney

🕐 TAKES 35 MINUTES   MAKES 1.8KG (4LB)   KEEPS FOR UP TO 1 YEAR

1 Combine all the ingredients except the sugar, salt, and dill or fennel in a large preserving pan. Bring the mixture to the boil, then reduce the heat to medium and simmer gently for 10–15 minutes until the vegetables begin to soften.

2 Add the sugar and salt, and continue to simmer for a further 15 minutes or so, until most of the liquid has evaporated.

3 Add the dill or fennel, and simmer for 2–3 minutes until the chutney has reached the desired consistency.

4 Pot into hot sterilized jars, seal, and label.

VARIATION
Other summer squash can be used here in place of courgettes – white, yellow, or pattypan squash work well. You can also use small round courgettes.

INGREDIENTS

1kg (2¼lb) firm medium courgettes, quartered lengthways, and cut into 1cm (½in) dice

4 large red onions, cut into 1cm (½in) dice

3 plump garlic cloves, crushed

75g (2½oz) fresh root ginger, finely chopped

2 tsp black mustard seeds

1 tbsp coarsely ground coriander seeds

500ml (16fl oz) cider vinegar

200g (7oz) golden sultanas

350g (12oz) white granulated sugar

1 tbsp salt

4 tbsp chopped fresh dill or fennel

Preserving tomatoes

MAKING THE MOST OF THE CROP

The delight of growing your own tomatoes is harvesting them, sweet and fresh, from the living plants in your garden or allotment – or, failing that, buying freshly picked ones from farmers' markets. Warehouse-ripened tomatoes cannot compare. Life is never that simple, though, and I often find that I have a mass of green, ripe, and overripe tomatoes all at the same time. Fortunately there are recipes that perfectly suit each stage of ripeness. All varieties can be used – look for the most plentiful crops.

Green tomatoes

A glut of green tomatoes gives you the perfect opportunity to stir up a batch of sharp and spicy green tomato chutney. These tomatoes have a higher than average acid content and are highly flavoured, but without the balancing sweetness of riper fruits. Look for mature, full-sized tomatoes that are beginning to turn slightly orange. Immature vine tomatoes are unsuitable for pickling, however, as they are not fully developed.

GREEN TOMATOES

RIPE TOMATOES

Ripe tomatoes

Use ripe tomatoes for lightly
cooked, chunky tomato
relishes. Look for firm flesh,
good aroma, and a wonderful
depth of colour. Ripeness can
be detected by smell, feel, and
taste, but don't be misled by
the scent of the calyx: this is
not an indication of flavour.

Overripe tomatoes

With their heady sweetness,
overripe tomatoes make
wonderful sauces and ketchups.
Vinegar replaces their lost
acidity. Do not confuse them
with rotten fruits, which smell
harsh and have almost liquid
flesh, and avoid any with mould.

OVERRIPE TOMATOES

Why relish and not chutney? Well, this side dish is lightly cooked to thicken it and, while it keeps well for 2–3 months if stored in the refrigerator, it hasn't enough sugar or vinegar to be stored on the larder shelf. The good news is that, unlike long-keeping chutneys that need time to mature, this relish is ready to serve at once.

Tomato and fennel hamburger relish

 TAKES 20 MINUTES  MAKES 750G (1½LB)   KEEPS FOR 2–3 MONTHS

1   Heat the oil in a stainless-steel or enamelled saucepan, add the onion and garlic, and fry over a low heat until softened.

2   Meanwhile, prepare the tomatoes. I leave the skins on for a chunky relish, but if you have a real aversion to the skins do peel them. To do this, score the tomatoes lightly on the base and immerse in a bowl of boiling water for a few seconds until the skins begin to loosen. Drain, return to the bowl, and cover with cold water to cool, then peel using a sharp knife.

3   Cut the tomatoes into 1cm (½in) dice, removing any stringy core. Add to the saucepan along with the sugar, vinegar, fennel seeds, salt, and pepper. Cook over a medium heat for 5–7 minutes until the mixture is thickish (it will thicken more as it cools).

4   Remove from the heat, and stir in the chopped fresh herbs. Pot the relish into hot sterilized jars, seal with vinegar-proof lids, and label. Store in the refrigerator.

VARIATION
If fennel is not your chosen spice, try coriander or mustard seeds instead – but remember that mustard seeds will add heat as well as flavour to the finished relish.

INGREDIENTS

2 tbsp olive oil

1 large red onion, chopped

2 plump garlic cloves, crushed

500g (1lb 2oz) ripe tomatoes

3 tbsp light muscovado sugar

3 tbsp white wine vinegar

1 tsp fennel seeds, crushed

1 tsp salt

a good quantity of freshly ground black pepper

2–3 tbsp chopped fresh coriander, tarragon, or basil

Look for tiny cherry-sized tomatoes for this relish and make sure they are just underripe. As ever the amount of chilli used is up to you. I have used only a small quantity, as this relish is a favourite with children. For a hotter, more fiery mix, increase the number of chillies and leave the seeds in, if wished. Serve with hamburgers, sausages, and kebabs.

Cherry tomato and onion relish

 TAKES I HOUR   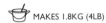 MAKES 1.8KG (4LB)    KEEPS FOR 6–9 MONTHS

1 Put the onions, chilli, and garlic in a preserving pan. Add the celery seed and vinegar and bring the mixture to the boil. Simmer for 15–20 minutes until the vegetables are cooked and most of the liquid has evaporated.

2 Add the tomatoes. Stir in the sugar and return to the boil. Simmer the relish over a moderate heat for 30 minutes or until the tomatoes soften and the relish thickens.

3 Remove from the heat and stir in the chopped basil.

4 Pot the relish into hot sterilized jars, cover with vinegar-proof seals, and label.

VARIATION
Although I have used white sugar because it gives a better flavour to this relish, raw sugar such as Demerara or muscovado can be used instead. You can also vary the spicing, using fennel seeds instead of celery seed, and chopped fresh mint in place of the basil.

INGREDIENTS

1kg (2¼lb) onions, chopped

1 fresh green chilli, deseeded if liked, and chopped

4 plump garlic cloves, crushed

1 tbsp celery seed

400ml (14fl oz) cider vinegar

1kg (2¼lb) cherry tomatoes, quartered if large

250g (9oz) white granulated sugar

good handful of chopped fresh basil

Rather more tasty and definitely less sweet than the commercial varieties, this family favourite can be made even more spicy with the addition of Tabasco sauce. If I have no ripe tomatoes on hand, I simply use good-quality Italian tinned plum tomatoes instead.

Tomato ketchup

🕐 TAKES 35 MINUTES   🍲 MAKES 2.25KG (5LB)   🥫 KEEPS FOR 6 MONTHS

1 For the spice mix, put all the ingredients in a coffee grinder and whiz until reduced to a powder, or grind using a mortar and pestle.

2 Put the tomatoes, onions, garlic, pepper, and celery in a large saucepan. Cover and cook gently over a medium heat for about 15 minutes until all the ingredients are very soft. Pass the mixture through a fine sieve or mouli.

3 Return the purée to the cleaned pan, and add the sugar, vinegar, and finely ground spice mix. Simmer for 20 minutes, stirring frequently, until the mixture thickens.

4 Remove from the heat and add the Tabasco sauce, if using. Pot into hot sterilized jars or bottles, seal with vinegar-proof lids, and label.

INGREDIENTS

3kg (6½lb) very ripe tomatoes

500g (1lb 2oz) onions, chopped

8 plump garlic cloves

1 large red pepper, deseeded and chopped

200g (7oz) celery, chopped

225g (8oz) golden granulated sugar

250ml (8fl oz) cider vinegar

½–1 tsp Tabasco sauce (optional)

FOR THE SPICE MIX

15 cloves

20 allspice berries

1 tsp celery seed

10cm (4in) cinnamon stick, broken into pieces

1 tbsp salt

1 tsp black peppercorns

VARYING THE CONSISTENCY

Thick or thin ketchup – the choice is yours. Vary the cooking time to achieve the consistency you like. You can also vary the spices according to what you enjoy. Coriander seed could replace the celery seed, while dark muscovado sugar would deepen the flavour.

At summer's end, I always have plenty of green tomatoes that seem resistant to ripening. This recipe makes such good use of them that it has become one of my storecupboard essentials. Serve this chutney with cheese, cold ham, and hot sausages.

Green tomato chutney

🕐 TAKES 1¼ HOURS   🍲 MAKES 2.5KG (5LB)   🥫 KEEPS FOR 6–9 MONTHS

1   Put the tomatoes, onions, and apples in a preserving pan with the vinegar. Simmer for about 30 minutes until the vegetables and apples are soft.

2   Meanwhile, prepare the chillies, removing the seeds, if wished, for a milder flavour. Transfer the chillies to a blender or food processor with the garlic and ginger, and whiz until you have a smoothish paste.

3   Add the paste to the pan with the raisins, sugar, and salt. Simmer over a low heat for 5 minutes, stirring, until the sugar has dissolved.

4   Increase the heat to medium, and continue to simmer the chutney for 30–40 minutes until thick.

5   Pot into hot sterilized jars, cover with vinegar-proof seals, and label.

INGREDIENTS

2kg (4½lb) green tomatoes, cores removed and sliced

750g (1lb 10oz) onions, chopped

500g (1lb 2oz) cooking apples, cored and finely chopped

600ml (1 pint) cider vinegar

4–6 red chillies, or to taste

6 plump garlic cloves

30g (1oz) fresh root ginger

225g (8oz) golden raisins or sultanas

500g (1lb 2oz) golden granulated sugar

2 tsp salt

CONTRASTING TEXTURES

Try to find large green tomatoes for this recipe – these give the best ratio of flesh to skin and seeds. Just-underripe ones also work well. Apples provide necessary bulk. Both these and the tomatoes will cook down, but the raisins retain their shape, adding extra flavour and texture.

A bright addition to any table, this relish is simple to make and looks wonderful. Try to use smallish beets for their intense flavour. Serve with pork, burgers, or cheese, especially Cheddar.

Beetroot and orange relish

 TAKES 1½ HOURS   MAKES 2.25KG (5LB)   KEEPS FOR UP TO 1 YEAR

1 Peel the beetroot and grate coarsely. This can be a messy procedure and the juice will stain both your hands and the chopping board, so it is best done in a food processor fitted with the appropriate blade. If grating the beetroot by hand, cover the work surface with a layer of newspaper, and wear rubber gloves to protect your hands.

2 Grate the zest from the oranges and set aside. Using a sharp knife, cut away all the white pith from the fruit. Cut the fruit into small dice, removing any pips and excess coarse membrane as you do.

3 For the spice mix, finely grind the cloves, cinnamon, allspice berries, and coriander seeds together in a spice mill or coffee grinder.

4 Put all the ingredients in a large preserving pan. Bring to the boil, stirring often to ensure that the sugar dissolves.

5 Reduce the heat and simmer for up to 1½ hours until the relish thickens, stirring frequently and taking care not to let the mixture catch and burn.

6 Pot into hot sterilized jars, seal with vinegar-proof lids, and label.

VARIATION
Using a muscovado sugar, light or dark, instead of the white sugar will give a deeper flavour to the finished relish.

INGREDIENTS

1kg (2¼lb) beetroot

4 large thick-skinned oranges

8 cloves

10cm (4in) cinnamon stick

20 allspice berries

1 tbsp coriander seeds

3 large onions, finely chopped

5cm (2in) piece of fresh root ginger, or 60g (2oz), grated

4 plump garlic cloves, crushed

600g (1lb 5oz) white granulated sugar

500ml (16fl oz) red wine vinegar

1 tbsp salt

This relish contains oil and so does not keep as well as other chutneys. Store in the refrigerator and use within two months. Serve with steak sandwiches, sausages, pies, and pork dishes.

Onion marmalade

🕐 TAKES 1 HOUR   🍲 MAKES 600G (1LB 5OZ)   🥫 KEEPS FOR 2 MONTHS

1 Finely slice the onions. Heat the oil in a large, deep frying pan and add the onions. Sweat over a low heat for 35–40 minutes, stirring frequently, until they have reduced considerably and are very soft. It is important not to allow the onions to brown, or the flavour of the marmalade will be too strong.

2 Once the onions have reduced, add the salt, sugar, vinegar, and thyme. Simmer until most of the liquid has evaporated and the marmalade is thick. Pot into hot sterilized jars, cover with vinegar-proof seals, and label. Store in the refrigerator.

INGREDIENTS

800g (1¾lb) red onions

4 tbsp olive oil

1 tsp salt

100g (3½oz) golden granulated sugar

5 tbsp red wine vinegar

1 tbsp fresh thyme leaves

Balsamic vinegar adds its characteristic sweetness to white wine vinegar in this unusual pickle.

Pickled garlic in balsamic vinegar

🕐 TAKES 10 MINUTES   🍲 MAKES 450G (1LB)   🥫 KEEPS FOR 6 MONTHS

1 Put the vinegars, sugar, salt, bay leaf, and spices in a saucepan over a low heat, and simmer for a few minutes until the sugar has dissolved.

2 Separate the garlic into cloves, peel, and add to the pan. Increase the heat and boil for 5 minutes. Drain, reserving the spiced vinegar.

3 Pack the garlic into hot sterilized jars. Pour over the vinegar, ensuring that the spices are evenly distributed and the garlic is covered: add more vinegar if necessary. Seal with vinegar-proof lids, and label. Store in a cool, dark place for 1 month before using. These garlic cloves sometimes form small brown spots on the surface, as do pickled onions, but the pickle is still edible.

INGREDIENTS

500ml (16fl oz) white wine vinegar

4 tbsp balsamic vinegar

60g (2oz) sugar

1 tsp salt

1 bay leaf

½ tsp coriander seeds

½ tsp white peppercorns

2–3 small dried red chillies

2–3 heads of garlic

Home-made pickled onions are far superior to ready-made ones, so settle down, switch on the radio, and get peeling. Choose small onions and buy them as soon as you see them – these tiny onions appear in the shops for a few brief weeks.

Pickled onions

🕐 NO COOKING   🍲 MAKES 1KG (2¼LB)   🗄 KEEPS FOR UP TO 1 YEAR

1 For the brine, put the salt in a large china or glass bowl. Pour over 300ml (10fl oz) boiling water, and stir to dissolve the salt. Add a further 1.2 litres (2 pints) cold water.

2 To make the onions easier to peel, bring a saucepan of water to the boil, then remove from the heat, tip in the onions, and leave for a few seconds. Taking one onion at a time, cut the tops and roots away, and remove and discard all the brown outer skin. Immediately immerse the peeled onion in the brine. As the onions are best peeled hot, you may need to pop the pan and its contents back on the heat for a few minutes should the skins become resistant.

3 Set the onions aside for 24 hours, to steep in the brine.

4 Make the spiced vinegar. Put the vinegar and spices in a saucepan, stir, and warm through for 3–4 minutes. The vinegar does not need to boil. Cover and set aside.

5 Drain the brined onions and wash well under cold running water. Pat dry using a clean tea towel or kitchen paper.

6 Pack the onions into cold sterilized jars, then pour in the spiced vinegar, ensuring that the onions are completely covered and adding more vinegar if required. I usually add some extra spices to each jar.

7 Seal with vinegar-proof lids, and store the onions in a cool, dark place. Check the onions after a couple of days to make sure they are still submerged in the vinegar. If necessary, top up with plain malt vinegar. Leave for at least 1 month before using.

INGREDIENTS

225g (8oz) salt

1kg (2¼lb) pickling onions

FOR THE SPICED VINEGAR

1 litre (1¾ pints) malt vinegar, plus extra if needed

1 bay leaf

6 cloves

2–3 mace blades

12 allspice berries

1 tbsp black peppercorns

1–2 dried red chillies (optional)

Pork pie without piccalilli; ploughman's lunch without piccalilli? Unthinkable! This is a classic pickle and a real favourite, and one that really is better home-made. Serve it with good hearty simple fare, such as grilled sausages, or cold meats and firm cheeses with crusty bread.

Piccalilli

🕐 TAKES 10 MINUTES   🥣 MAKES 2KG (4½LB)   🥫 KEEPS FOR 6 MONTHS

1 For the brine, put the salt in a large china or glass bowl. Pour over 450ml (15fl oz) boiling water and stir to dissolve the salt. Add a further 1.7 litres (3 pints) cold water. Add the vegetables and leave to soak overnight.

2 For the sauce, combine the flour, mustard, sugar, and turmeric in a large bowl. Add a little of the vinegar and work into a paste, adding more vinegar if required. Mix in the remaining vinegar, and pour into a large preserving pan.

3 Bring the mixture to the boil, whisking constantly. Continuing to whisk, simmer for 4–5 minutes until the sauce is thick and smooth. Remove from the heat.

4 Rinse the vegetables and drain well. Add all the vegetables to the sauce, bring back to the boil, and simmer for about 3 minutes until they are cooked but still a little crisp.

5 Pot into hot sterilized jars, pressing the vegetables down to ensure that they are covered and adding extra vinegar if needed. Seal with vinegar-proof lids, and label.

VARIATION

This mixed vegetable pickle offers an excellent way to make the most of a late summer glut. Cauliflower and pickling onions are essential ingredients, but some people also include carrots. French beans can replace the runner beans.

INGREDIENTS

225g (8oz) salt

450g (1lb) pickling onions

1 medium cauliflower, broken into small florets

225g (8oz) runner beans, sliced into 2.5cm (1in) lengths

2 ridged cucumbers or courgettes, diced

2 heads of plump garlic cloves

FOR THE SAUCE

30g (1oz) plain flour

60g (2oz) mustard powder

225g (8oz) white granulated sugar

1 tbsp ground turmeric

750ml (1¼ pints) distilled malt vinegar, plus extra if needed

This rich brown pickle is almost but not quite a chutney. It has a mix of vegetables and is lightly cooked in a rich sweet and spicy sauce. It's perfect with crusty bread and cheese, but good, too, with cold meats and in sandwiches.

Ploughman's pickle

🕐 TAKES 30 MINUTES   🥘 MAKES 3.6KG (8LB)   🥫 KEEPS FOR 6 MONTHS

1   For the brine, put the salt in a large china or glass bowl. Pour over 300ml (10fl oz) boiling water and stir to dissolve the salt. Add a further 1.2 litres (2¼ pints) cold water. Add the vegetables and leave to soak overnight.

2   The following morning, drain the vegetables and rinse well under cold running water. Lay on a clean tea towel to drain.

3   Meanwhile, put the apples and garlic in a large preserving pan with 300ml (10fl oz) of the vinegar. Simmer for 10 minutes or until soft. Remove from the heat.

4   In a bowl, mix the cornflour with about 4 tablespoons of the vinegar into a smooth paste, and set aside.

5   Add the remaining vinegar, sugar, and spices to the pan, including the cayenne, if using. Bring the mixture to the boil, stirring until the sugar dissolves. Stir a few spoonfuls of the hot liquid into the cornflour mix, then add to the pan. Stir constantly while the mixture thickens until you have a smooth sauce.

6   Simmer for 2–3 minutes, then add the drained vegetables. Bring to the boil, then simmer for 5 minutes. Take care with this pickle, as it burns easily on the bottom.

7   Pot into hot sterilized jars, seal with vinegar-proof lids, and label.

INGREDIENTS

225g (8oz) salt

1 large cauliflower, broken into florets

750g (1lb 10oz) firm courgettes, cut into 1cm (½in) dice

2 large onions, cut into 1cm (½in) dice

1 celery heart, cut into 1cm (½in) dice

450g (1lb) cooking apples, cored and diced

4 or 5 plump garlic cloves, crushed

1 litre (1¾ pints) distilled malt vinegar

60g (2oz) cornflour

675g (1½lb) dark muscovado sugar

1 tbsp ground cinnamon

1 tbsp ground turmeric

1 tbsp ground cumin

1 tsp ground nutmeg

1 tsp allspice

¼ tsp cayenne pepper (optional)

To avoid diluting the concentration of the vinegar in this pickle, the cucumbers must be leached of their excess liquid. Salting rather than brining is used here, as the water content of the cucumbers is high. Eat with hot dogs, hamburgers, and deli sandwiches.

Bread and butter pickle

⏱ TAKES 15 MINUTES   🍲 MAKES 1KG (2¼LB)   🥫 KEEPS FOR UP TO 3 MONTHS

1 Arrange the vegetables in a shallow bowl, and sprinkle with the salt. Toss lightly with a fork to coat. Leave overnight.

2 The following morning, drain the vegetables, rinse under cold running water, then spread out on clean tea towels to drain.

3 In a large preserving pan or stainless-steel saucepan, combine the vinegar, sugar, and spices. Bring this mixture to the boil, then simmer for 10 minutes.

4 Add the drained vegetables and boil for 1 minute. Remove with a slotted spoon.

5 Pack the vegetables into hot sterilized jars, and pour over the hot pickling liquid. Make sure that the vegetables are completely immersed in the liquid, adding extra vinegar if needed. Seal with vinegar-proof lids, and label. Store in a cool, dark place. Once opened, store in the refrigerator.

INGREDIENTS

2 large or 4–6 small cucumbers, deseeded if large, and sliced

1 green pepper, deseeded and finely sliced

1 large mild onion, finely sliced

50g (1¾oz) salt

400ml (14fl oz) cider vinegar, plus extra if needed

200g (7oz) white granulated sugar

1 tsp ground turmeric

1 tsp celery seed, coarsely crushed

1 tsp mustard powder

1 tsp fennel seeds, coarsely crushed

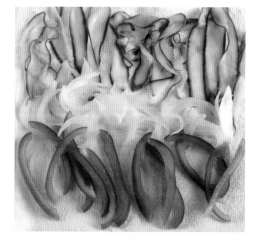

CAREFUL PREPARATION

Look for firm cucumbers and choose ones that are on the small side, as these will hold less water. When preparing the cucumbers, pepper, and onion, try to cut everything evenly and very finely. The finished pickle with benefit from this extra care, making it well worth the time and effort.

This is a cabbage pickle that can be made in a dozen different ways. I like to salt the vegetables, then cook them in the seasoned vinegar. You can make up your own spice mix adding fennel, dill, coriander seeds, or finely grated fresh root ginger.

Chow chow

 TAKES 20 MINUTES  MAKES 2KG (4½LB) ⊟ KEEPS FOR 3–6 MONTHS

1   In a large china or glass bowl, arrange the vegetables in layers, sprinkling each layer with salt. Cover with a dry cloth and leave in a cold place for 12 hours.

2   Drain the vegetables and rinse well under cold running water. Spread out on a clean dry tea towel to drain.

3   Put the vegetables, vinegar, sugar, and spices in a large preserving pan. Bring the mixture to the boil, then simmer for 20 minutes.

4   Pack into hot sterilized jars, packing the mixture down firmly with a teaspoon. Seal with vinegar-proof lids, and label. Store in the refrigerator. The chow chow will be ready for use after 1 week.

VARIATION
Grated carrot, red pepper, or even a small quantity of red cabbage could be used to make a more colourful pickle.

INGREDIENTS

1kg (2¼lb) shredded white cabbage

600g (1lb 5oz) mild white onions

2 green peppers, deseeded and finely sliced

60g (2oz) salt

1 litre (1¾ pints) white wine vinegar

100g (3½oz) white granulated sugar

3 tbsp black mustard seeds, lightly crushed

2 tbsp celery or dill seeds, lightly crushed

This pickle is flavoured with curry seasonings, rather than curried as such. I use a spoonful or two of bought curry paste, but you could use curry powder or your own masala mix. Work the powder into a paste with a little vinegar and the sugar before adding the remaining liquid.

Curried cauliflower and carrot pickle

🕐 TAKES 30–40 MINUTES    MAKES 1.5KG (3LB 3OZ)   🗄 KEEPS FOR 6 MONTHS

1 For the brine, combine the salt with 1 litre (1¾ pints) very cold water in a large bowl or jug.

2 Put the vegetables in a large glass or china bowl. Pour over the brine, cover, and leave to soak in a cool place for at least 6 hours or preferably overnight.

3 Drain and rinse well under cold running water. Spread the vegetables out on a clean tea towel to dry.

4 Combine the vinegar, sugar, and curry paste or powder in a large preserving pan. Add the bay leaves and bring to the boil. Add the drained vegetables and simmer the mixture for 10–15 minutes. The vegetables should still retain some crispness. Drain the vegetables, reserving the spiced vinegar.

5 Pack the vegetables into hot sterilized wide-mouthed jars, and spoon over the vinegar, ensuring that the vegetables are covered and adding extra vinegar if necessary.

6 Seal with vinegar-proof lids and label. Stored in a cool, dark place, the pickle will be ready for use after 4 weeks. The spices may sink to the bottom, so gently invert the jars before use.

INGREDIENTS

45g (1½oz) salt

750g (1lb 10oz) small cauliflower florets

500g (1lb 2oz) carrots, sliced

100g (3½oz) onion, finely sliced

1 litre (1¾ pints) distilled malt vinegar, plus extra if needed

125g (4½oz) golden granulated sugar

1–2 tbsp curry paste or powder

2 bay leaves

These mushrooms are crisp, sweet, and salty, and excellent as an antipasto. Buy small button mushrooms and prepare as soon as possible. Remember that mushrooms soak up water like sponges; don't wash them, but rather brush them with a soft brush or dust with kitchen paper.

Pickled mushrooms

 TAKES 25 MINUTES   MAKES 900G (2LB)   KEEPS FOR 3 MONTHS

1   Put all the ingredients except the mushrooms in a preserving pan and stir to combine. Bring to the boil, then reduce the heat and simmer over a medium heat for 5 minutes.

2   Add the mushrooms to the pan, and cook at boiling point for a further 10 minutes.

3   Using a slotted spoon, remove the mushroom mixture from the pan, reserving the pickling liquid. Pack the mixture into hot sterilized jars.

4   Continue to boil the pickling liquid for 5–10 minutes until it has reduced by one-third. Pour over the mushrooms, ensuring that they are completely covered. Use extra vinegar if needed.

5   Seal with vinegar-proof lids, label, and store in the refrigerator.

VARIATION

If you collect wild mushrooms, they can be preserved in this fashion. Do be certain, though, that all the fungi are edible – mistakes can be unpleasant or even toxic. Use a reputable identification guide, or ask an expert. Clean wild mushrooms carefully, as they often contain grit, as well as tiny wildlife.

INGREDIENTS

500ml (16fl oz) white wine vinegar, plus extra if needed

2 garlic cloves, sliced

1 medium shallot, sliced

1 tbsp coriander seeds, coarsely crushed

1 tsp black peppercorns, coarsely crushed

1 tbsp dried oregano

1 tbsp white granulated sugar

½ tsp salt

750g (1lb 10oz) button mushrooms, trimmed

*You can adapt this recipe for any quantity. If the beets are small, cut them into quarters.
If large, I find slices work best. Beetroot will stain anything it comes into contact with, including
your hands, so it is wise to wear rubber gloves when preparing.*

Pickled beetroot

🕐 TAKES UP TO 1 HOUR   🥘 MAKES 1.8KG (4LB)   🥫 KEEPS FOR 6 MONTHS

1 Put the beetroot in a large saucepan and cover with cold water.
Bring to the boil, then simmer for 15 minutes for baby beets and up
to 1 hour for larger ones, or until they are cooked through. Drain
and set aside.

2 Meanwhile, in a stainless-steel or enamelled saucepan, combine the
vinegar and all the spices except for the chillies, and bring to the boil.
Turn off the heat and set aside.

3 As soon as the beets are cool enough, slip off the skins. (I always
wear gloves to do this, as the beets will stain your hands quite
dramatically.) Quarter or slice the beets, and pack them into hot
sterilized jars, slipping a few chillies down the sides if liked.

4 Strain the vinegar and pour over the beets. For a more spicy pickle,
don't strain the vinegar, but pour directly onto the beets, ensuring
that the spices are evenly divided among the jars. The beets should
be covered with vinegar, so add extra if necessary.

5 Seal with vinegar-proof lids, label, and store in a cool, dark place for
1 week before using.

INGREDIENTS

1kg (2¼lb) raw beetroot, trimmed

1 litre (1¾ pints) distilled malt vinegar, plus extra if needed

2–3 mace blades

1 cinnamon stick

1 bay leaf

1 tbsp black peppercorns

12 allspice berries

1–2 dried red chillies (optional)

VARIATION
Try adding some dill – either the crushed seeds or the fresh herb – to
the vinegar in this recipe. Coriander combined with the finely grated
zest of an orange also works well.

This rather old-fashioned pickle is still a favourite – and almost worth making for its beautiful colour alone. My best memories of this pickle stem from my childhood. I can still picture the big bowls of salted cabbage waiting in our larder for my mother to continue with the job.

Pickled red cabbage

  TAKES 5–10 MINUTES   MAKES 2KG (4½LB)   KEEPS FOR UP TO 1 YEAR

1 Cut the cabbage in half and remove any coarse outer leaves. With a sharp knife, cut away the central stem and discard. Slice the cabbage as finely as possible.

2 Arrange the vegetables in alternate layers in a large china bowl, scattering the salt between the layers. Set aside and leave overnight.

3 Meanwhile, pour the vinegar into a saucepan and add the spices. Bring the mixture up to boiling point, stir in the sugar, then turn off the heat, cover the pan, and leave overnight.

4 The following day, wash the cabbage and onion mixture under cold running water to remove all the salt. Drain in a colander, then spread on clean old tea towels to dry for about 1 hour.

5 Pack the cabbage into cold sterilized jars, pressing the cabbage down well. Pour in the vinegar, ensuring that each jar contains some of the spices and that the vinegar covers the vegetables. Top up with extra vinegar if needed.

6 Seal with vinegar-proof lids, label, and store in a cool, dark place for at least 4 weeks before using.

INGREDIENTS

1kg (2¼ lb) red cabbage

2 red onions, finely sliced

1–2 tbsp salt

FOR THE SPICED VINEGAR

1 litre (1¾ pints) distilled malt vinegar, plus extra if needed

3 mace blades, lightly crushed

1 cinnamon stick, lightly crushed

6 cloves, lightly crushed

12 allspice berries, lightly crushed

2–3 tbsp Demerara sugar

I like to include dill flowers in this pickle for their aniseed-like flavour. Pick them from the garden and add to the vinegar mix. Serve these beans with antipasti, or cold roast meats.

Pickled green beans with garlic

 TAKES 20 MINUTES   MAKES 1KG (2¼LB)   KEEPS FOR 3–6 MONTHS

1 Top and tail the green beans, and cut them in half. Chop the chilli. Separate the garlic into cloves, and peel. Put all the ingredients except the beans in a preserving pan and bring to the boil. Simmer for 5 minutes. Add the beans and simmer for a further 5 minutes.

2 Drain the mixture, reserving the vinegar, and spoon into hot sterilized jars.

3 Return the vinegar to the heat, and boil for 10 minutes or until reduced by about one-third. Pour over the beans, making sure that they are completely covered and adding extra vinegar if needed.

4 Seal with vinegar-proof lids, and label. Store in a cool, dark place. Once opened, store in the refrigerator.

INGREDIENTS

600g (1lb 5oz) green beans

1 dried red chilli

1–2 heads of garlic

1 litre (1¾ pints) distilled malt vinegar

1 tsp salt

50g (1¾oz) golden granulated sugar

1 tsp coriander seeds

1 tbsp allspice berries

2–4 bay leaves

This may also be made with tiny pickling onions. Allow to mature for 4 weeks before using.

Sweet chilli pickled shallots

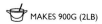 NO COOKING   MAKES 900G (2LB)   KEEPS FOR UP TO 1 YEAR

1 For the brine, put the salt in a large china or glass bowl. Pour over 300ml (10fl oz) boiling water and stir to dissolve the salt. Add a further 1.2 litres (2 pints) cold water.

2 Meanwhile, place the shallots in a bowl and cover with boiling water. Leave for 5 minutes, then drain and peel. Separate the garlic into cloves; peel. Soak the shallots and garlic in the brine overnight.

3 Crush the chillies. Heat the vinegar, sugar, bay leaves, and chillies in a stainless-steel or enamelled saucepan, then leave to infuse overnight.

4 Drain and rinse the shallots and garlic. Pack into hot sterilized jars, pour over the vinegar, seal with vinegar-proof lids, and label.

INGREDIENTS

225g (8oz) salt

1kg (2¼lb) shallots

1 head of garlic

4 dried red chillies

1 litre (1¾ pints) distilled malt vinegar

3 tbsp light muscovado sugar

3 bay leaves, crushed

These tangy little cucumbers are good with pâtés, cold meats, and sandwiches. They can also be chopped into sauces such as tartare and gribiche, a type of mayonnaise.

Pickled gherkins

 TAKES 15 MINUTES   MAKES 750G (1LB 10OZ)   KEEPS FOR 6–9 MONTHS

1 For the brine, dissolve the salt in 1 litre (1¾ pints) water in a large bowl. Pour into a stainless-steel or enamelled saucepan.

2 Wash the gherkins and add to the brine. Bring the mixture to the boil and simmer for 10 minutes.

3 Meanwhile, in another stainless-steel or enamelled saucepan, combine the vinegar, bay leaves, and spices, and warm this mixture over a low heat for about 5 minutes, stirring.

4 Lift the gherkins from the brine using a slotted spoon, rinse, then pack into hot sterilized jars. Pour over the vinegar, ensuring that the spices are evenly divided among the jars and that the gherkins are covered. Add extra vinegar if required.

5 Seal with vinegar-proof lids, label, and store in a cool, dark place for 1 month before using.

INGREDIENTS

115g (4oz) salt

500g (1lb 2oz) small, firm gherkins

500ml (16fl oz) white wine or distilled malt vinegar, plus extra if needed

2 bay leaves

1 tsp white peppercorns

6 cloves

½ tsp allspice berries

1 tsp fennel or dill seeds

Orchard fruit

Cooking apples • Crab apples • Dessert apples
Dried fruits • Figs • Medlars
Pears • Quinces

Rather a boozy dessert preserve, spiced pears are a useful storecupboard standby. Use smallish pears and do make sure you have the fruit completely submerged in the liquid to ensure a good result. Serve with cream, ice cream, or – best of all – chocolate cake and cream.

Pears in white wine with lemongrass

🕐 TAKES 40 MINUTES   🍲 MAKES 1.4KG (3LB)   🫙 KEEPS FOR 6 MONTHS

1   Cut away 20cm (8in) of the hard root end of the lemongrass and discard. Slice the stem finely. Using a rolling pin, give the remaining top part of the stem a good bash, along with the ginger, to release the flavour.

2   In a large preserving pan, combine the wine, honey, sugar, sliced and crushed lemongrass, chilli, ginger, lime leaves if using, and lemon zest and juice. Bring the syrup to the boil and simmer for 5 minutes, stirring until the sugar has dissolved.

3   Peel the pears, but retain their stalks. Add the pears to the syrup in the pan, and poach gently for 20 minutes or until just cooked through. Remove the pears, and pack into hot sterilized jars.

4   Boil the syrup until thick. Divide among the jars, topping up with brandy or vodka, ensuring that the pears are covered. You may need to top up again after a couple of weeks. Seal, label, and store in a cool, dark place for 1 month before using.

INGREDIENTS

4 stalks lemongrass

2.5cm (1in) piece of fresh root ginger

1 bottle white wine

100g (3½oz) honey

450g (1lb) white granulated sugar

1 red chilli, deseeded if liked, and sliced

4–6 lime leaves, available from Asian stores (optional)

finely grated zest and freshly squeezed juice of 2 lemons

12–14 firm, ripe dessert pears

brandy or vodka, to cover

COOKING AND FLAVOURING

These pears become quite soft during cooking, so don't worry about how they will fit into your jars. If you prefer a milder flavour, omit the chilli and lemongrass, and use a cinnamon stick and 1 or 2 star anise instead.

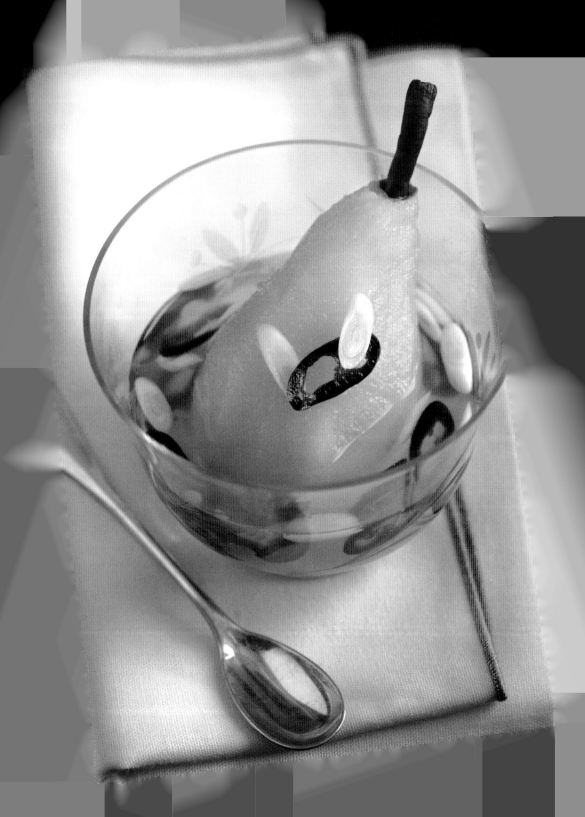

Choose firm, ripe pears with a good flavour for this conserve. I like to use Comice or Williams Bon Chrétien. The crystallized ginger adds a surprise element to this unusual recipe.

Pear, apple, and ginger conserve

 TAKES 25 MINUTES    MAKES 1.25KG (2¾LB)   KEEPS FOR 6 MONTHS

1 Peel and core the pears and apples, and cut into chunks. Put all the ingredients in a large preserving pan, and simmer over a medium heat, stirring from time to time, until the sugar has dissolved.

2 Increase the heat and boil the mixture for 15 minutes or until the apples have softened, then test for a set.

3 Once setting point has been reached, pot the conserve into hot sterilized jars, seal, and label.

INGREDIENTS

900g (2lb) firm pears

600g (1lb 5oz) cooking apples

115g (4oz) crystallized ginger, finely chopped

600g (1lb 5oz) white granulated sugar

juice of 2 lemons

grated zest of 1 lemon

Pretty and pink – what more can you ask of a jelly? Crab apples are small enough to be cooked whole, but if there are any bruised or bad patches simply cut these away.

Crab apple jelly

 TAKES 50 MINUTES    MAKES 1KG (2¼LB)   KEEPS FOR 6–9 MONTHS

1 Put the apples and 1.2 litres (2 pints) water in a large preserving pan. Add the lemon rind, ginger, and cinnamon. Bring to the boil, then cover the pan and simmer for 30–40 minutes until the apples have collapsed and are pulpy. Spoon the mixture into a jelly bag and leave to drip for 6–12 hours.

2 Measure the juice and weigh out the correct amount of sugar. Put the sugar and juice in the cleaned preserving pan, and bring slowly to the boil, stirring until the sugar has dissolved. Cook at a full rolling boil for 5 minutes, then test for a set.

3 When the jelly has reached setting point, pot into hot sterilized jars, seal, and label.

INGREDIENTS

1.5kg (3lb 3oz) crab apples

pared rind of 1 lemon

5cm (2in) piece of fresh root ginger, crushed

20cm (8in) cinnamon stick

500g (1lb 2oz) white granulated sugar for each 600ml (1 pint) juice

I'm often asked for a recipe that uses up a glut of apples. This easy preserve can be used in many different ways – spread on buttered toast, stirred into sauces, or served with roast meat.

Apple butter

 TAKES 3 HOURS    MAKES 2KG (4½LB)   KEEPS FOR UP TO 1 YEAR

1   Put the apples and 450ml (15fl oz) water in a large heavy pan, and simmer for 45–60 minutes until the mixture forms a thick purée.

2   Wrap all the spices loosely in a muslin bag. Add to the purée with the sugar and stir well. Simmer over a very low heat, stirring to dissolve the sugar, for up to 1½ hours. The purée will become very thick and dark in colour. If possible, place the pan on a heat diffuser to prevent the mixture from sticking and therefore burning.

3   To test that the butter is ready, allow a spoonful to cool on a plate. When it is ready, it will hold its shape (see p19).

4   Remove the spice bag, pot into hot sterilized jars, seal, and label.

VARIATION
For a simpler, more subtle flavour, make this apple butter without the spices. Alternatively, you could use the crushed seeds from 6–8 cardamom pods, instead of the cloves.

INGREDIENTS

1.8kg (4lb) cooking apples, peeled, cored, and roughly chopped (prepared weight)

6 cloves, crushed

½ nutmeg, crushed

10cm (4in) cinnamon stick, crushed

5cm (2in) piece of fresh root ginger, crushed

1.35kg (3lb) white granulated sugar

Preserving with apples

CHOOSING FRUIT

Apples are one of the most useful fruit for making jams and jellies, chutneys, and relishes. They add bulk and can provide pectin, as well as adding acidity to your preserves. To tell if apples are ripe for picking, gently cradle the fruit in your hand and rock it. If the stem separates from the tree, the fruit is ripe. If the apple remains firmly attached, try another day. Use windfalls at once and store hand-picked apples for future use in a cold, dry, dark place.

Types and uses

It is not always necessary to have first rate, unbruised apples. Cut away broken or bruised areas and discard any with insect infestation. Never use an apple that has any trace of mould anywhere, as this might affect the preserve's keeping qualities. Overripe apples and those that have been stored can be used, but their acidity will be low. Apples fall into three groups:

Eating (dessert) apples tend to hold their shape during cooking and include Golden Delicious, Cox's, and Spartan.

Cooking apples break down during cooking and include Bramley, Red Delicious, and Gravenstein.

Crab apples are small and therefore time-consuming to prepare, so are best used for making jelly or added to other jams or jellies to increase yield.

GRAVENSTEIN

COOKING APPLES
These are most often used to add bulk to preserves, but cooking apples are also perfect for making apple butter.

RED DELICIOUS

BRAMLEY

GOLDEN DELICIOUS

SPARTAN

EATING APPLES add both flavour and a chunky texture to preserves, as they hold their shape rather than breaking down to form a pulp.

COX'S

Easy to produce and so useful to have in the larder, cinnamon apple jelly can be made from windfall apples or just a bargain buy at the market. Sour cooking apples are best, as dessert apples tend to hold their shape when cooked and in this recipe we're looking for a purée.

Cinnamon apple jelly

 TAKES 1–1½ HOURS  MAKES 1.25KG (2¾LB) ⬚ KEEPS FOR UP TO 1 YEAR

1 Put the apples and 1 litre (1¾ pints) water in a large preserving pan. Add the lemon rind, ginger, and cinnamon. Bring to the boil, then cover the pan and simmer for 1 hour or until the apples have collapsed and are pulpy.

2 Spoon the mixture into a jelly bag and leave to drip for 6–12 hours.

3 Measure the juice and weigh out the correct quantity of sugar. Put the sugar and juice in the cleaned preserving pan, and bring the mixture slowly to the boil, stirring until the sugar has dissolved. Increase the heat and cook at a full rolling boil for 10 minutes, then test for a set.

4 When the jelly has reached setting point, remove any scum from the surface with a slotted spoon. Pot the jelly into hot sterilized jars. (You can put a piece of cinnamon stick in each jar before adding the jelly, if liked.) Seal and label.

VARIATION
Orange rind and cloves can replace the lemon rind and cinnamon here. The richer flavour they add is particularly good with hot buttered toast.

INGREDIENTS

1.5kg (3lb 3oz) cooking apples, diced

thinly pared rind of 1 lemon

5cm (2in) piece of fresh root ginger, crushed

20cm (8in) cinnamon stick, roughly broken, plus extra if wished (see method)

500g (1lb 2oz) white granulated sugar for each 600ml (1 pint) juice

Medlars are an acquired taste. Hard when harvested, they need to be kept in a dark place for 6–8 weeks to soften until almost rotten. If you have a medlar tree in your garden, they fruit prolifically. This jelly makes the best use of them. Serve with game, meat pies, and terrines.

Medlar jelly

🕐 TAKES I HOUR   🍲 MAKES 1.5KG (3LB 3OZ)   📦 KEEPS FOR UP TO I YEAR

1 Put the medlars and I litre (1¾ pints) water in a large preserving pan, and simmer for 30–40 minutes until the fruit is very soft.

2 Spoon the mixture into a jelly bag and allow to drip overnight.

3 Measure the juice: you will have approximately I litre (1¾ pints). Weigh out the appropriate amount of sugar. Pour the juice into the cleaned preserving pan, and add the sugar and lemon juice.

4 Bring the mixture slowly to the boil, stirring often, until the sugar has dissolved. Cook at a full rolling boil for 2–3 minutes.

5 Add the pectin. Return the mixture to the boil and cook for a further minute before testing for a set.

6 When the jelly has reached setting point, pot into hot sterilized jars, seal, and label.

INGREDIENTS

2kg (4½lb) medlars

85g (3oz) white granulated sugar for each 100ml (3½fl oz) juice

freshly squeezed juice of 3 lemons

125g (4½oz) liquid pectin

VARIATION
While it is true that medlars have a pronounced flavour all their own, adding a 10cm (4in) piece of fresh root ginger, peeled and finely grated, at the same time as you add the sugar, works well in this recipe.

This recipe comes from the traditional cuisine of the Western Cape region of South Africa and makes wonderful use of green — that is, unripe — figs. When cooked, the fruits turn a deep, translucent bottle-green. Serve with thinly sliced, buttered white bread, or with desserts.

Green fig preserve

🕐 TAKES UP TO 2¼ HOURS   🍲 MAKES 1KG (2¼LB)   🍯 KEEPS FOR 6 MONTHS

1 In a large glass or china bowl, dissolve the salt in 2 litres (3½ pints) water to make the brine.

2 Cut a small cross in the base of each fig and scrape the skins if they are very furry. Put the prepared figs in the brine, and leave to soak for 24 hours.

3 Drain the figs and rinse under cold running water. Put in a saucepan, cover with water, and add the bicarbonate of soda. Bring to the boil and simmer for 10–15 minutes until the figs are just tender. Drain.

4 Meanwhile, make the syrup. Put the sugar and 300ml (10fl oz) water in a preserving pan and bring to the boil. Add the ginger. Simmer for about 5 minutes until the syrup thickens slightly.

5 Lift the figs into the syrup, and simmer gently over a low heat for 1–2 hours until the fruit are translucent.

6 Drain the figs, reserving the syrup. Pack the fruit into hot sterilized jars and cover with the syrup, discarding the ginger. Seal and label.

VARIATION
To give this preserve an extra kick, add a few mild fresh green chillies, deseeded and sliced, at the same time as you add the ginger. Discard before potting.

INGREDIENTS

100g (3½oz) salt

1kg (2¼lb) unripe green figs

1 tsp bicarbonate of soda

FOR THE SYRUP

1kg (2¼lb) white granulated sugar

10cm (4in) piece of fresh root ginger, lightly crushed

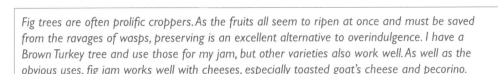

Fig trees are often prolific croppers. As the fruits all seem to ripen at once and must be saved from the ravages of wasps, preserving is an excellent alternative to overindulgence. I have a Brown Turkey tree and use those for my jam, but other varieties also work well. As well as the obvious uses, fig jam works well with cheeses, especially toasted goat's cheese and pecorino.

Fig jam

🕐 TAKES 45 MINUTES 🍲 MAKES 1.35KG (3LB) 🥫 KEEPS FOR 6 MONTHS

1 Cut the hard stems from the tops of the figs and peel. Cut the flesh into 1cm (½in) chunks.

2 Put the figs, lemon juice, and zest in a large preserving pan. Simmer over a low heat for about 30 minutes until the figs are very soft.

3 Add the sugar and continue to simmer over a low heat, stirring, until the sugar has dissolved.

4 Stir in the pectin, increase the heat, and cook at a full rolling boil for 10 minutes, then test for a set.

5 When the jam has reached setting point, pot into hot sterilized jars, seal, and label.

INGREDIENTS

1.1kg (2½lb) ripe figs

freshly squeezed juice of 2 lemons

finely grated zest of 1 lemon

1kg (2¼lb) white granulated sugar

125g (4½oz) liquid pectin

RETAINING THE PIPS

Like raspberry jam, fig jam contains a large number of pips. I think this is an important part of its character and so prefer not to sieve these out. If your preference is for a smooth preserve, however, you could rub the mixture through a fine sieve once the sugar has dissolved, but before you add the pectin.

Quince trees take several years to mature, but once they begin to fruit you are assured of the essential ingredient for this delicious preserve, also known as membrillo. *My recipe has been adapted from* The Boston Cooking School Cookbook *published in the 19th century.*

Quince cheese

🕐 TAKES UP TO 3 HOURS   🍲 MAKES 1.25KG (2¾LB)   🥫 KEEPS FOR UP TO 3 YEARS

1 Cut the quinces into chunks about 4cm (1¾in) in size. Put in a saucepan and cover with water. Simmer for 30 minutes, partially covered, until the quinces are very soft. You may need to add more water. Alternatively, wrap the quinces in foil and bake in a 180°C (350°F/Gas 4) oven for about 1 hour until they are soft.

2 Mash the fruit roughly, and rub through a fine sieve to produce a smooth purée.

3 Put the purée in a heavy preserving pan with the sugar and lemon juice. Simmer over a low heat for 20 minutes, stirring frequently, until the sugar has dissolved.

4 Increase the heat to medium and simmer, stirring frequently, until the purée is very thick. It will darken slightly. Watch carefully as this preserve can catch and burn.

5 Pot the cheese into hot sterilized jars, seal, and label.

INGREDIENTS

1kg (2¼lb) quinces

900g (2lb) white granulated sugar

freshly squeezed juice of 3 lemons

CHOOSING FRUIT

I try to find the largest quinces around for this preserve, as they cook much more quickly than the small, hard ones found on my bushes. Don't worry about any small blemishes on the fruit – just cut them away.

A real autumn relish this – the plums add both sharpness and rich seasonal colour.
Relying on fresh spices rather than dried ones, this preserve has a light, refreshing flavour.
It goes especially well with cold meats, grilled pork chops, or mature cheeses.

Apple, plum, and onion relish

 TAKES I HOUR    MAKES 1.6KG (3½LB)   KEEPS FOR UP TO I YEAR

1   Using the small bowl of a food processor or a mortar and pestle, work the garlic, ginger, and chillies into a paste.

2   Put all the ingredients except the sage in a preserving pan, and bring to the boil, stirring, until the sugar has dissolved.

3   Over a fairly low heat, simmer the relish for 40 minutes or until it is reduced and thickish. Stir in the sage and continue to simmer for a further 2–3 minutes, until it has reached the desired consistency.

4   Pot the relish into hot sterilized jars, cover with vinegar-proof seals, and label. Store in a cool, dark place.

VARIATION
While I have chosen to use red plums here, a glut of yellow plums would be a perfect alternative for use in this relish.

INGREDIENTS

5 plump garlic cloves

10cm (4in) piece of fresh root ginger

2 green chillies, deseeded if liked, and chopped

1kg (2¼lb) cooking apples, peeled, cored, and chopped

675g (1½lb) sweet onions, peeled and chopped

500g (1lb 2oz) red plums, stoned and chopped

360ml (12fl oz) cider vinegar

300g (10oz) white granulated sugar

1 tbsp salt

2 tbsp chopped fresh sage

Using two different types of apple produces the characteristic chunkiness of this classic sauce.

Chunky apple sauce

 TAKES 30 MINUTES    MAKES 1.6KG (3½LB)   KEEPS FOR 3 MONTHS

1   Peel, core, and roughly chop the cooking apples. Put in a large preserving pan with 400ml (14fl oz) water and simmer for 10 minutes, or until the apples soften and break down to a purée.

2   Meanwhile, peel, core, and cut the dessert apples into 1cm (1½in) dice. Add to the cooking apples with the sugar and lemon juice. Bring the mixture to the boil, and simmer for 20 minutes until there is little excess liquid and the sauce is thick.

3   Pot into hot sterilized jars, seal, label, and store in a cool, dark place.

INGREDIENTS

1kg (2¼lb) cooking apples

4 firm dessert apples

300g (10oz) white granulated sugar

freshly squeezed juice of 2 lemons

This is a wonderfully useful chutney, made from Orchard fruit and the last of the tomatoes.

Pear, apple, and tomato chutney

 TAKES 1¼ HOURS    MAKES 2.5KG (5½LB)   KEEPS FOR UP TO 1 YEAR

1   To skin the tomatoes, cut a cross in the base of each one and immerse for 1–2 minutes in a bowl of boiling water. When the skins start to loosen, drain the tomatoes, peel, and chop the flesh. Chop the onions. Peel, core, and chop the apples and pears. Crush the garlic, and grate the ginger. Deseed the chillies if liked, and chop.

2   Put all the ingredients in a preserving pan, and bring slowly to the boil, stirring until the sugar has dissolved. Increase the heat to medium, and simmer the chutney for 1¼ hours or until thick.

3   Pot in hot sterilized jars, cover with vinegar-proof seals, and label.

INGREDIENTS

675g (1½lb) ripe tomatoes

450g (1lb) onions

1.25kg (2¾lb) cooking apples

500g (1lb 2oz) firm pears

4–6 garlic cloves

100g (3½oz) fresh root ginger

1–2 red chillies

450g (1lb) raisins

1 tbsp salt

900ml (1½ pints) white wine vinegar

750g (1lb 10oz) Demerara sugar

This lovely recipe comes from my mother and is a good way to use up windfall apples.

Easy apple and onion chutney

 TAKES I HOUR    MAKES 3.6KG (8LB)   KEEPS FOR UP TO I YEAR

1 Peel, core, and chop the apples. Chop the onions, garlic, and ginger. Deseed the chilli if liked, and chop. Put the apples, onions, garlic, ginger, and chilli in a large preserving pan. Pour in the vinegar and stir in the sugar, turmeric, and salt.

2 Bring the mixture to the boil, stirring until the sugar has dissolved, then simmer for about I hour until thick. Stir often as the mixture reduces, to avoid it catching on the bottom of the pan and burning.

3 Spoon into hot sterilized jars, cover with vinegar-proof seals, label, and store in a cool, dark place for about I month before using.

INGREDIENTS

1.8kg (4lb) cooking apples

900g (2lb) onions

3–4 plump garlic cloves

60g (2oz) fresh root ginger

I large red chilli

I litre (1¾ pints) distilled malt vinegar

550g (1¼lb) light muscovado sugar

2 tbsp ground turmeric

I tbsp salt

Relatively smooth, this tasty, tangy chutney is perfect for cheese and cold meat sandwiches.

Curried apple and date chutney

 TAKES 1¼ HOURS    MAKES 4.5KG (10LB)   KEEPS FOR UP TO I YEAR

1 Peel, core, and quarter the apples. Chop the onions, dates, ginger, and garlic. Put all the ingredients except the sugar in a large preserving pan and simmer for 20 minutes over a medium heat until the apples have begun to soften. Add the sugar and simmer for a further 5 minutes, stirring occasionally, until the sugar has dissolved.

2 Increase the heat and boil the chutney 45–50 minutes, stirring often, until well reduced and thick.

3 Pot into hot sterilized jars, cover with vinegar-proof seals, and label.

INGREDIENTS

2kg (4½lb) cooking apples

6 large onions

500g (1lb 2oz) stoned dates

10cm (4in) piece fresh root ginger

4–8 plump garlic cloves

2 tbsp salt

I litre (1¾ pints) malt vinegar

2–3 tbsp Madras curry paste

1kg (2¼lb) light muscovado sugar

Choose whatever combination of dried fruit suits your taste – such as dates, apricots, figs, peaches, raisins – but try to make it as varied as possible. The chutney takes very little time to cook, as the high proportion of dried fruit helps it to thicken quickly.

Storecupboard chutney

 TAKES UP TO 1 HOUR    MAKES 1KG (2¼LB)   KEEPS FOR UP TO 1 YEAR

1   Cut the larger dried fruit into even-sized pieces, about 1cm (½in) in size.

2   Put the dried fruit, apples, onions, garlic, ginger, chillies, sugar, and salt in a large heavy preserving pan. Add the vinegar and stir so that all the ingredients are well combined.

3   Bring the mixture to the boil, reduce the heat, and simmer for 30–45 minutes, stirring occasionally, until the mixture has reached the desired consistency.

4   Pot into hot sterilized jars, cover with vinegar-proof seals, and label. Store in a cool, dark place.

VARIATION

Apples add the bulk and fresh flavour here, but any other fruit, if found in plentiful supply, can be used instead, such as pears, plums, or mangoes.

INGREDIENTS

675g (1½lb) mixed dried fruit

1.35kg (3lb) cooking apples, peeled and chopped

2 large onions, chopped

6 plump garlic cloves, chopped

5cm (2in) piece of fresh root ginger, grated

1–2 dried red chillies, crushed

675g (1½lb) light muscovado sugar

1 tbsp salt

1 litre (1¾ pints) cider or distilled malt vinegar

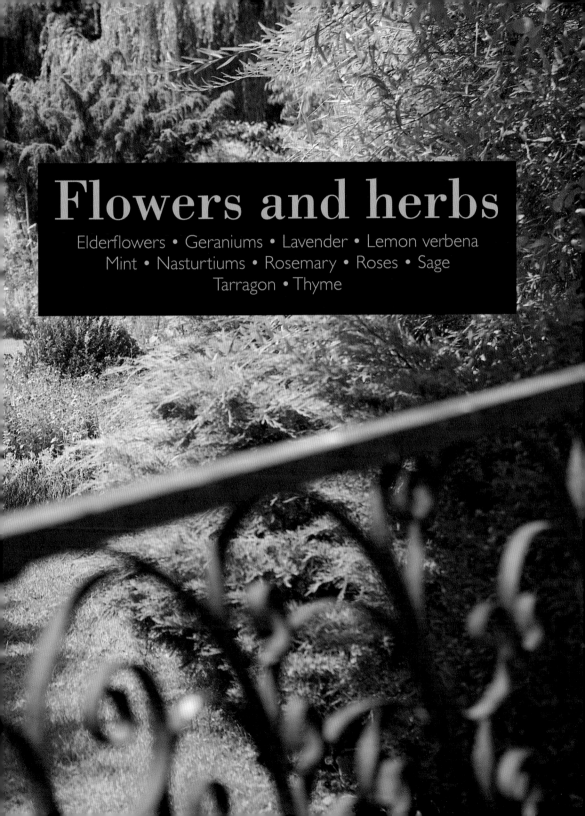

Flowers and herbs

Elderflowers • Geraniums • Lavender • Lemon verbena
Mint • Nasturtiums • Rosemary • Roses • Sage
Tarragon • Thyme

Pink rose petals suspended in clear pink, wine-flavoured jelly, fragranced with rose water, make this one of the prettiest and most unusual of all preserves. Rose waters differ in strength; try to find a full-bodied one for this recipe. This jelly is delicious with scones for afternoon tea, or served with breakfast in bed on Valentine's Day.

Rosé wine and rose petal jelly

🕐 TAKES 20 MINUTES 🍲 MAKES 1.25KG (2¾LB) 📦 KEEPS FOR 9–12 MONTHS

1 In a preserving pan, combine the wine with the sugar. Stir the mixture over a low heat until the sugar has completely dissolved. Increase the heat and bring the mixture to a full rolling boil. Boil for 2 minutes, skimming off any scum that rises to the surface.

2 Remove from the heat and stir in the pectin and rose water. Return the mixture to heat and bring back to the boil. Boil for 1 minute.

3 Add the rose petals and pot the jelly into hot sterilized jars. Place the lids lightly on top, and allow the jelly to set for about 15 minutes.

4 Using a sterilized metal spoon, gently stir the petals down into the setting jelly.

5 Once the jelly has set, tighten the lids and label the jars.

INGREDIENTS

750ml (1¼ pints) rosé wine

800g (1¾lb) white granulated sugar

175g (6oz) liquid pectin

4 tbsp rose water

2 handfuls of unsprayed rose petals

CHOOSING AND PICKING PETALS

Small rose petals work well in this recipe. They should be freshly picked, dry, and unblemished. Match the petals to the colour of the wine. Pale pink ones will best be complemented by a delicately coloured rosé, while for a richer, more jewel-like hue, try a Shiraz rosé with petals from a deep red damask rose.

Flavoured with scented geranium leaves, this jelly is evocative of summer days in the garden Rose-scented leaves are especially good. For extra tanginess, add the juice of 2 lemons.

Scented geranium leaf jelly

🕐 TAKES 50 MINUTES   🍲 MAKES 1.25KG (2¾LB)   🗄 KEEPS FOR 6–9 MONTHS

1 Put the apples and 1 litre (1¾ pints) water in a large preserving pan. Add the geranium leaves and bring to the boil. Cover and simmer for 40 minutes, or until the apples have collapsed and are pulpy. Spoon the mixture into a jelly bag and leave to drip for 6–12 hours.

2 Measure the resulting liquid and weigh out the correct quantity of sugar. Put the sugar and juice in the cleaned preserving pan. Bring slowly to the boil, stirring until the sugar has dissolved. Increase the heat and cook at a full rolling boil for 10 minutes, then test for a set.

3 When the jelly has reached setting point, pot into hot sterilized jars, placing a couple of small leaves on top of the jelly. Seal and label.

INGREDIENTS

1.5kg (3lb 3oz) cooking apples

12 geranium leaves, plus extra to decorate

500g (1lb 2oz) white granulated sugar for each 600ml (1 pint) juice

---

This sophisticated crystal-clear jelly is as simple to make as it is delicious to eat. Serve with cold meats, pork roasts, and at celebration meals with roast duck or goose.

Sage and sauternes jelly

🕐 TAKES 10 MINUTES   🍲 MAKES 1.25KG (2¾LB)   🗄 KEEPS FOR 6–9 MONTHS

1 In a preserving pan, combine the wine and sugar, and stir over a low heat until the sugar has dissolved. Increase the heat and bring the mixture to a full rolling boil, and boil for 2 minutes.

2 Turn off the heat and stir in the pectin. Bring the mixture back to the boil and boil for 1 minute, then test for a set.

3 Once the jelly has reached setting point, add the leaves and flowers, if using, and allow to settle for 10 minutes before potting into hot sterilized jars. Leave for a further 15 minutes, covered, stirring the herbs down into the jelly with a sterilized metal spoon if necessary. Seal and label.

INGREDIENTS

750ml (1¼ pints) Sauternes or other sweet white wine

800g (1¾lb) white granulated sugar

250g (9oz) liquid pectin

handful of small fresh sage leaves, finely sliced

1 tbsp unsprayed sage flowers (optional)

This adaptable herb jelly is perfect with roast lamb, and is also delicious on toast. Using apples as a base, it is scented with both rosemary stems and flowers.

Rosemary jelly

 TAKES 50 MINUTES   MAKES 1.35KG (3LB)   KEEPS FOR 6–9 MONTHS

1   Put the apples and 1 litre (1¾ pints) water in a large preserving pan and add the rosemary sprigs. Bring the mixture to the boil, cover the pan, and simmer for 40 minutes or until the apples have collapsed and are pulpy.

2   Spoon the mixture into a jelly bag, and leave to drip for at least 6 hours or preferably overnight.

3   Measure the juice and weigh out the correct quantity of sugar. Put both in the cleaned preserving pan and bring to the boil, stirring frequently, until the sugar has dissolved.

4   Once the sugar has dissolved, increase the heat and cook the jelly at a full rolling boil for 5–10 minutes, skimming off any scum that rises to the surface, then test for a set.

5   When the jelly has reached setting point, add the rosemary flowers, if using, and simmer for a further 30 seconds.

6   Allow the jelly to cool for about 5 minutes, before stirring gently with a sterilized metal spoon to distribute the flowers. Pot into hot sterilized jars, seal, and label.

VARIATION
Other herbs can be used here in place of the rosemary: sage, thyme, and marjoram all work well.

INGREDIENTS

1.5kg (3lb 3oz) cooking apples, peeled, cored, and diced

6–8 sprigs of fresh rosemary, roughly chopped

500g (1lb 2oz) white granulated sugar for each 600ml (1 pint) juice

handful of unsprayed rosemary flowers (optional)

Few herbs are more evocative of the scented summer garden than lavender. Here, it adds its fragrance to a pretty jelly, just right for an elegant tea. Blackberries provide colour; if you want a more jewel-like hue, use a few drops of red food colouring as well.

Lavender jelly

🕐 TAKES UP TO I HOUR   🍲 MAKES I.5KG (3LB 3OZ)   🥫 KEEPS FOR 6–9 MONTHS

1 Put the apples, blackberries, 2 tablespoons of the lavender flowers, and 1.7 litres (3 pints) water in a large preserving pan. Simmer for 40–50 minutes until the apples are very soft.

2 Put the pulp in a jelly bag and allow to drip for several hours. Don't be tempted to squeeze the bag, as the jelly will be clouded if you do.

3 Measure the resulting juice and weigh out the correct quantity of sugar. Put the juice, sugar, a few drops of food colouring, if using, and the remaining flowers in the cleaned preserving pan. Bring slowly to the boil. Cook at a full rolling boil for 5 minutes, skimming off any scum that rises to the surface, then test for a set.

4 Once the jelly has reached setting point, pot into hot sterilized jars, seal, and label.

INGREDIENTS

1.8kg (4lb) cooking apples, cored, and diced

a few blackberries, to colour

3 tbsp unsprayed lavender flowers

450g (1lb) white granulated sugar for each 600ml (1 pint) juice

red food colouring (optional)

CHECKING THE FLOWERS

Always check flowers before you use them to see that they are not harbouring any insects, and do smell the flowers, too – the flavour is scent-related, so a dull scent equals a dull preserve. Most importantly, remember to ensure that the flowers are actually edible, and avoid any flowers that have been sprayed with pesticides.

Preserving with flowers and herbs

PICKING AND PREPARING

Using flowers and herbs to flavour and season preserves links us with the apothecaries and herbalists of history. Gather your flowers and herbs early on a dry day. Flowers should be just at the point of full bloom before any wilt begins. With larger blooms, check for insect activity and gently tap the flowers to dislodge unwanted inhabitants. If your herbs and flowers are clean, dust-free, and growing out of range of pet activity, there is no need to wash them — although you must be very sure they have not been sprayed with any pesticides. If they are gritty, or a pesticide suitable for use on edible crops has been used, you must rinse them thoroughly. Lay on clean dry tea towels to dry fully before use.

BAY LEAVES are useful for flavouring sugars, vinegars, and other savoury preserves.

ROSE PETALS, from buds on the point of opening, are best for jellies and sugars. Choose varieties with small petals and use soon after picking.

LAVENDER is most heady when the florets are deeply coloured and not quite open. Dry on a clean tea towel in the sun for 2–3 days if not using at once.

ROSEMARY is a strongly scented herb. Use the soft, small shoots, and try to include some of the flowers – they taste delicious,

MINT comes in many varieties. Choose the small, newer leaves and remove all the coarse stems before chopping. Use at once.

LEMONGRASS is a popular flavouring in Southeast Asian cuisine. The pale green stalks can be used to impart a lemony tang to preserves.

GERANIUM and other scented leaves, such as lemon verbena and blackcurrant, can add flavour to vinegars and sugars to good effect.

THYME has a distinctive flavour and should be picked and used in the same way as rosemary.

BASIL should, if possible, be the small-leaved Greek type, as it has an intense scent without too much water in the leaves.

SAGE can add flavour to jellies and sugars. Use the soft end shoots, and flowers if available.

A traditional accompaniment to lamb, this jelly is easy to make and stores well. You can add a few drops of green food colouring to the jelly if you want to, but I like to leave it natural.

Mint jelly

 TAKES 20 MINUTES   MAKES 1KG (2¼LB)   KEEPS FOR 6 MONTHS

1 Using a food processor, finely chop the lemon shells. Put in a heavy saucepan with 750ml (1¼ pints) water, and bring to the boil. Simmer for 15 minutes, then leave to strain through a jelly bag for 2 hours.

2 Measure the liquid and make it up to 500ml (16fl oz). Pour this into a preserving pan, and add the sugar and vinegar. Stir over a low heat until the sugar has dissolved.

3 Increase the heat and cook at a full rolling boil for 3 minutes, then test for a set.

4 When the jelly has reached setting point, stir in the mint. Pot the jelly into hot sterilized jars, cover with vinegar-proof seals, and label.

INGREDIENTS

shells from 4 lemons
(see p208)

500g (1lb 2oz) sugar

6 tbsp white wine vinegar

2 good handfuls of fresh
mint, finely chopped

You may already have a jar of vanilla sugar on the shelf, but why not prolong the sweetness of summer by making aromatic sugars with herbs and flowers? Lavender must be my favourite. Lemon verbena, rose, thyme, bay, and rosemary also work well, but I find sage a little antiseptic.

Sweet herb sugars

 NO COOKING   MAKES 250G (9OZ)   KEEPS FOR UP TO 1 YEAR

1 Fill one-third of a sterilized jar with sugar, and sprinkle with some of the herbs or flowers. Build up alternate layers in this way until the jar is full. Repeat with any other jars.

2 Seal, label, and leave to infuse for at least 1 week before using. If liked, you can sieve the sugar before using to remove the herbs or flowers, but as I often like to include them in my recipes I prefer to leave the sugar unsieved.

INGREDIENTS

250g (9oz) refined caster
sugar

a good handful of
unsprayed herbs or
flowers, such as lavender
flowers, rosemary leaves
or flowers, thyme leaves,
lemon verbena leaves

Green tea has wonderful antioxidant properties. Whether they are present in this jelly I can't say, but I like to think that something that is both fragrant and delicious must be good for you.

Green tea and lime jelly

 TAKES 10 MINUTES   MAKES 1KG (2¼LB)   KEEPS FOR 6 MONTHS

1   Put the tea leaves, lime zest, and a few jasmine flowers in a large glass bowl. Pour over 1 litre (1¾ pints) boiling water and leave to infuse for 1–2 hours.

2   Strain the tea into a stainless-steel or enamelled saucepan, and add the lime juice and sugar. Stir over a low heat until the sugar has dissolved, then add the pectin, stirring well.

3   Increase the heat and bring the mixture to the boil. Cook at a full rolling boil for 2–3 minutes, skimming off any scum that rises to the surface, then test for a set.

4   When the jelly has reached setting point, stir in the extra jasmine flowers. Allow to cool for about 10 minutes, then pot the jelly into hot sterilized jars, seal, and label.

VARIATION
Edible jasmine flowers are available from specialist suppliers of the type that also sell green teas, rosebuds, etc. If you cannot find any, omit the jasmine flowers and use 2 tablespoons loose jasmine tea leaves, or a green tea and jasmine mix, instead.

INGREDIENTS

1–2 tbsp green tea leaves

finely grated zest of
3 limes

a few unsprayed jasmine flowers, plus extra to decorate

freshly squeezed juice of
2 large limes

750g (1lb 10oz) white granulated sugar

125g (4½oz) liquid pectin

Herb vinegars are a wonderful addition to the cook's repertoire of flavours. I like to scent vinegar with tarragon, a soft herb that does not dry well. Pick it early in the morning on a dry day when it will be fullest in flavour and when insect activity is at its lowest. Use good-quality vinegar: both white wine and cider vinegars are excellent.

Tarragon vinegar

🕐 NO COOKING   🍲 MAKES 360ML (12FL OZ)   📦 KEEPS FOR 1 YEAR

1　Put the tarragon in a glass bowl with the vinegar. Cover the bowl tightly with two layers of cling film, and leave the vinegar to infuse for 7 days in a cool, dark place.

2　Strain the vinegar, then pour it into a sterilized bottle. Push in a couple of strands of the freshly picked tarragon, and close the bottle with a vinegar-proof seal.

3　Store the vinegar in a cool, dark place.

VARIATION

This simple recipe can be adapted for use with other herbs, according to preference and availability. Try making it with fresh chervil or basil instead of tarragon. A selection of herb vinegars on your shelves will be a good storecupboard standby.

INGREDIENTS

a good handful of fresh dry tarragon, roughly chopped, plus extra freshly picked, unsprayed tarragon

360ml (12fl oz) white wine or cider vinegar

This wonderfully fragrant cordial is so easy to make and so delicious in summer drinks, fruit salads, sorbets, and jellies. Pick elderflowers first thing in the morning, shaking gently to remove any wildlife. To minimize the risk of the cordial fermenting, it is essential that you use spotlessly clean utensils. Citric acid is available from Asian, Polish, and Jewish grocery stores.

Elderflower cordial

🕐 TAKES 5 MINUTES   🍲 MAKES 1.7 LITRES (3 PINTS)   🗄 KEEPS FOR 6 MONTHS

1 Put the sugar and 1.7 litres (3 pints) water in a large saucepan, and boil for 5 minutes, stirring occasionally, to dissolve the sugar.

2 Chop the lemons, oranges, and limes into 2.5cm (1in) cubes. Put in a large, spotlessly clean glass or china bowl with the dry flowerheads. Pour over the hot syrup, stir in the citric acid, and cover with a clean cloth. Leave the bowl in a cool, dark place for 4 days, stirring each day with a clean spoon.

3 Strain the syrup through scalded muslin, and pour into sterilized bottles. Seal and label. Store in the refrigerator. To serve, dilute the cordial to taste.

VARIATION

For a more tart, refreshing drink, replace one of the oranges with two extra limes – perfect for cooling you down on a hot summer's day.

INGREDIENTS

1kg (2¼lb) white granulated sugar

2 organic or unwaxed lemons

2 organic or unwaxed oranges

4 organic or unwaxed limes

about 20 large elderflower heads (see p152)

60g (2oz) citric acid

Pretty in the garden, nasturtiums are also useful in the kitchen. The flowers are both delicious and attractive in salads, and the seed pods can be pickled and used like capers. However, the plants are rather prone to blackfly. If you need to spray them, make sure you use a spray that is not harmful when eaten. Pick young berries before the pods yellow and the seeds harden.

Pickled nasturtium berries

 NO COOKING  MAKES 400G (14OZ) KEEPS FOR 6 MONTHS

1 To make the brine, combine the salt and 500ml (16fl oz) water in a large glass or china bowl, stirring until the salt has dissolved.

2 Add the berries and leave them to soak for 24 hours, then drain well and set aside.

3 In a saucepan, combine the vinegar, bay leaves, dill, and peppercorns, and bring to the boil. Once the vinegar is boiling, turn off the heat.

4 Pack the nasturtium berries into a hot sterilized jar, and pour over the hot herb vinegar. Seal with a vinegar-proof lid, and store in a cool, dark place. Leave for 4 weeks before using.

VARIATION
A few green peppercorns sprinkled into the vinegar with the white peppercorns adds a lovely flavour to this unusual pickle.

INGREDIENTS

50g (1¾oz) salt

1 teacup of nasturtium berries with short stems

250ml (8fl oz) white wine vinegar

2 bay leaves

a few sprigs of fresh dill

½ tsp white peppercorns, lightly crushed

Wild harvest

Blackberries • Chestnuts • Cloudberries • Elderberries
Juniper berries • Rosehips • Rowan berries • Horseradish
Samphire • Sloes • Walnuts

This is one of the easiest jams to make and a great favourite with my mother-in-law Nancy Prince, who had an orchard and a few blackberry bushes. Apples are rich in pectin and acid, while blackberries add colour and extra flavour. This jam is delicious spooned over rich Greek-style yogurt.

Bramble and apple jam

🕐 TAKES 40 MINUTES   🍲 MAKES 1.25KG (2¾LB)   🫙 KEEPS FOR UP TO 1 YEAR

1   Put the apples and blackberries in a preserving pan with the lemon juice and 200ml (7fl oz) water. Simmer over a low heat for about 30 minutes until the apples have collapsed and are pulpy, and the sugar has dissolved. Mash with a wooden spoon.

2   Increase the heat and cook the mixture at a full rolling boil for 10 minutes, then test for a set. Using a slotted spoon, skim off any scum that has formed on the surface of the jam.

3   Once the jam has reached setting point, pot into hot sterilized jars, seal, and label.

INGREDIENTS

1kg (2¼lb) cooking apples, peeled, cored, and chopped

300g (10oz) blackberries

freshly squeezed juice of 1 lemon

1kg (2¼lb) white granulated sugar

MAKING THE MOST OF WINDFALLS

This recipe produces a beautiful jewel-coloured firm preserve. As this is essentially a jam made from windfall apples and wild berries, you do not need to worry if the apples are bruised – simply cut away any blemishes. The final result will still be delicious.

Ripe elderberries and blackberries may be gathered from hedgerows in late summer or early autumn. Wash the fruit in warm water to make sure that it has no dust or animal residue on it.

Wild berry jam

🕐 TAKES 40 MINUTES   🍲 MAKES 1.6KG (3½LB)   🥫 KEEPS FOR 6–9 MONTHS

1   Put the plums in a bowl with 250g (9oz) sugar, and leave for 2–4 hours to draw out the juice.

2   Put the berries and 100ml (3½fl oz) water in a preserving pan, and simmer for 15–20 minutes until the fruit is soft. For a smoother jam, press through a coarse sieve. Return to the pan. Add the plums, the remaining sugar, the vinegar, and the lemon juice.

3   Simmer over a low heat until the sugar has dissolved. Increase the heat and cook the mixture at a full rolling boil for 10–15 minutes, then test for a set.

4   Once the jam has reached setting point, pot into hot sterilized jars, seal, and label.

INGREDIENTS

1kg (2¼lb) purple plums, stoned, and coarsely chopped

1.35kg (3lb) white granulated sugar

1kg (2¼lb) mixed elderberries and blackberries

1 tbsp cider vinegar

freshly squeezed juice of 1 lemon

These beautiful berries confuse the novice picker because they are red when unripe and golden when ripe. They grow in the Northern Hemisphere and have a raspberry-like flavour.

Cloudberry jam

🕐 TAKES 20 MINUTES   🍲 MAKES 600G (1LB 5OZ)   🥫 KEEPS FOR 6 MONTHS

1   Put the berries in a preserving pan, with just the water remaining on them after washing. Heat slowly until the berries soften, then boil for 5 minutes. Add the sugar and continue to cook, stirring, until the sugar has dissolved.

2   Stir in the pectin and lemon juice. Increase the heat and cook at a full rolling boil for 2 minutes, then test for a set.

3   Once the jam has reached setting point, pot into hot sterilized jars, seal, and label.

INGREDIENTS

500g (1lb 2oz) cloudberries, hulled and washed

325g (11oz) white granulated sugar

125g (4½oz) liquid pectin

freshly squeezed juice of 1 lemon

Brambles are the cultivated blackberry's wild cousins. Picking the berries may result in thorn-scratched arms and fingers, but this delicious jelly more than makes up for the experience.

Bramble jelly

🕐 TAKES 30 MINUTES   🍲 MAKES 1.25KG (2¾LB)   🥫 KEEPS FOR 9 MONTHS

1 Put the berries, apples, and 500ml (16fl oz) water in a preserving pan. Simmer the mixture for 10 minutes, then spoon into a jelly bag and allow to drip overnight.

2 Measure the juice and weigh out the correct quantity of sugar. Pour the juice into the cleaned preserving pan, and add the sugar. Cook over a medium heat, stirring, until the sugar has dissolved.

3 Increase the heat and cook at a full rolling boil for 3 minutes, then test for a set.

4 Once the jelly has reached setting point, pot into hot sterilized jars, seal, and label.

INGREDIENTS

1kg (2¼lb) wild blackberries, washed

2 large cooking apples, chopped

100g (3½oz) white granulated sugar for each 100ml (3½fl oz) juice

---

This pretty pink jelly is delicious with hot buttered toast or crumpets. Resist the temptation to squeeze the bag as the juice drips or the resulting jelly will be cloudy.

Rosehip jelly

🕐 TAKES 50 MINUTES   🍲 MAKES 1KG (2¼LB)   🥫 KEEPS FOR 6 MONTHS

1 Wash the rosehips and remove the stalks. Put in a preserving pan with 1 litre (1¾ pints) water, and simmer for 40 minutes, or until the rosehips are soft. Transfer to a jelly bag; allow to drip for 12 hours.

2 Measure the juice: you should have about 900ml (1½ pints). Put in a preserving pan with the sugar, lemon juice, and pectin. Bring the mixture slowly to the boil, stirring to dissolve the sugar, then cook at a full rolling boil for 2 minutes. Test for a set.

3 Once the jelly has reached setting point, pot into hot sterilized jars, seal, and label.

INGREDIENTS

1kg (2¼lb) rosehips

750g (1lb 10oz) white granulated sugar

freshly squeezed juice of 2–3 lemons, about 120ml (4fl oz)

250g (9oz) liquid pectin

Foraging for wild food

BEFORE YOU BEGIN

When setting off on a walk with foraging in mind, the first question you must ask yourself is: "Am I legally allowed to forage for food here?" It is essential that you make sure you are not trespassing or taking away plants that are protected on otherwise open land. Don't be greedy – just take your share and leave the rest for others, and for the plants themselves to regenerate.

Choosing and picking

You will need a knife, basket, brown paper bags, punnets for fruit, and appropriate clothing made of sturdy material for tackling bramble bushes and protecting you from other prickly plants. A good pair of gardening gloves is also handy.

Elderflowers (see p144) are at their best picked in the early morning before the insects get busy. Choose youngish blooms with a heady fragrance.
Wild berries such as rowan berries and blackberries should be gathered on dry days and picked from only those boughs above dog level.

Horseradish needs to be dug up, so a small fork is useful. Leave some of the root so that the plant can regrow.
Samphire should be picked when small, and pulled directly from the mud.
Nuts should be within easy reach – otherwise you must wait until the nuts fall.

ROSEHIPS High in vitamin C and iron, the plump red hips from the dog rose, Rosa Canina, are found in abundance from mid summer.

ROWAN Often used by herbalists, rowan berries have a high content of both vitamins A and C. They make wonderful jellies.

BLACKBERRIES Cousin of the domestic cultivar, wild blackberries have an intense flavour. They should be gathered early in the autumn before the fruit withers.

Packed with vitamin C, rosehip syrup makes a delightful cordial. Gather the rosehips from hedgerow roses, and choose fully ripe red hips. You can tell if they are ready for picking by squeezing them gently: they should give slightly to the touch. Rosehip syrup is delicious spooned over creamy desserts, such as vanilla ice cream, or diluted with water as a late summer drink.

Rosehip syrup

🕐 TAKES 1–1¼ HOURS   🍲 MAKES 1.2 LITRES (2 PINTS)   🫙 KEEPS FOR 6 MONTHS

1 Bring 1.5 litres (2¾ pints) water to the boil in a large preserving pan. Meanwhile, mince the rosehips in either a mincer or food processor, and transfer immediately to the boiling water.

2 Bring the mixture back to the boil and allow to stand for 15 minutes. Pour into a jelly bag, and allow it to drip overnight or until most of the liquid has come through. Reserve the pulp.

3 In the cleaned preserving pan, bring 750ml (1¼ pints) fresh cold water to the boil. Stir in the pulp, turn off the heat, and let stand for 10 minutes. Pour into the cleaned jelly bag, and allow to drip for 2–3 hours.

4 Combine the two juices in a large bowl. Clean and wash the jelly bag thoroughly and pour the juices through once more.

5 Transfer the juices to the cleaned preserving pan and boil to reduce the liquid until it measures about 900ml (1½ pints). Add the sugar and boil for a further 5 minutes.

6 Pour into hot sterilized bottles, seal, and label.

INGREDIENTS

1kg (2¼lb) rosehips

600g (1lb 5oz) white granulated sugar

COOKING AND STRAINING

To retain as much of the hips' vitamin content as possible, you must have the boiling water ready so you can plunge the hips into it as soon as you have minced them. The rosehip and water mixture needs to be strained through the bag twice to ensure that all the tiny irritating fibres are removed.

Gathering wild chestnuts is a wonderful autumn pastime, but do check that you are free to do so. In many countries, even trees along main roads have owners who may object if you help yourself to their bounty. Don't worry if the nuts break when you are peeling them — they will still taste delicious. Serve with ice cream, or add to chocolate cakes and puddings.

Candied chestnuts

 TAKES 30 MINUTES  MAKES 1KG (2¼LB)   KEEPS FOR UP TO 1 YEAR

1 Make a small cut through the hard outer skin of each chestnut. Put the prepared nuts in a large saucepan, cover with water, and bring to the boil. Simmer for 10 minutes, then remove from the heat.

2 Using a slotted spoon, lift the chestnuts from the water one at a time, and peel off both the hard outer skin and the papery brown inner skin. From time to time, you will need to reheat the water, as the nuts peel much more easily when hot.

3 Put the sugar, 500ml (16fl oz) water, and vanilla in a stainless-steel or enamelled saucepan, and stir over a low heat for 5 minutes until the sugar has dissolved. Bring the mixture to the boil, then simmer for 3–4 minutes.

4 Add the chestnuts and boil for a further 10 minutes. Tip the syrup and nuts into a large glass or ceramic bowl, and leave to stand for at least 12 hours.

5 Split open the vanilla pod, scrape out the seeds, and add the seeds to the nuts and syrup.

6 Return the nuts and syrup to the cleaned preserving pan, bring to the boil, and simmer for 1 minute. Transfer to the glass or ceramic bowl, and leave for 24 hours.

7 Cook again as in step 6, then pot the mixture into hot sterilized jars, seal, and label.

INGREDIENTS

1kg (2¼lb) sweet chestnuts

1kg (2¼lb) white granulated sugar

1 vanilla pod

The nuts must be pickled before the shells have started to form. To test this, prick each one with a needle at the end opposite the stem, and discard it if you feel any resistance. Each nut must also be pricked to allow the brine to sink in. A silver fork was once used as old-fashioned steel would taint the flavour, but modern stainless steel is fine. Serve with cheese or cold meats.

Pickled walnuts

 NO COOKING   MAKES 1.5KG (3LB)   KEEPS FOR UP TO 1 YEAR

1   To make the brine, dissolve half the salt in 500ml (16fl oz) water in a large bowl. It helps the salt to dissolve if you heat a little of the water first, and immerse the salt in that. Top up with the remaining cold water, and allow to cool. Brine should always be used cold to prevent bacterial growth.

2   Prick the walnuts all over with a fork, then add to the brine, ensuring that they are submerged: weigh down with a plate if necessary. Leave for 5 days.

3   Make a fresh batch of brine as above with the remaining salt and another 500ml (16fl oz) water. Drain the walnuts, submerge in the new brine, and leave for a further 7 days.

4   Drain the walnuts again and spread, in a single layer, on a tray to dry. I like to do this outside if the weather is kind. Turn the nuts often and leave until they are uniformly black. This will take 2–3 days.

5   The day before you are due to pot the walnuts, make the spiced vinegar. Combine the vinegar and spices in a stainless-steel or enamelled saucepan, and bring to the boil. Add the sugar, stir well, and leave for 24 hours to infuse.

6   When you are ready to pot the walnuts, strain the spiced vinegar into a clean stainless-steel or enamelled saucepan, and bring back to the boil to reheat. Pack the walnuts into hot sterilized jars, pushing them down well. Cover with the hot spiced vinegar, then cover the jars with vinegar-proof seals, and label. Leave for at least 3 months to mature before using.

INGREDIENTS

450g (1lb) salt

1 kg (2¼lb) walnuts, shelled and pricked with a silver or stainless-steel fork

FOR THE SPICED VINEGAR

1 litre (1¾ pints) malt vinegar

1 tbsp coriander seeds, crushed

12 allspice berries

2–3 red chillies, deseeded if liked

75g (2½oz) light muscovado sugar

Sloes are traditionally picked after the first frost. Given today's climatic vagaries, I put my sloes into the freezer for a couple of days. This helps the skins to break down more easily. It also frees you to make the gin at a time convenient to you, as sloes freeze well for up to a year.

Sloe gin

 NO COOKING  MAKES 900ML (1½ PINTS)  KEEPS FOR 1–3 YEARS

1 Pick over the sloes, discarding any that are grubby or have become mouldy. Now freeze at least overnight or for up to 1 year.

2 When you are ready to make the gin, defrost the sloes. You now have two options for preparing them. You may prick them with a silver or stainless-steel fork (old-fashioned steel would taint the flavour). Alternatively, put them into the goblet of a food processor and press the pulse button once or twice. I choose the latter method, but have friends who swear only hand-pricking each sloe makes the best gin.

3 Put the prepared sloes in a large china or glass bowl, and pour over the gin, reserving the bottle for later use. Stir in the sugar. Cover the bowl with two or three layers of cling film, and leave in a cool, dark place for 2–3 months.

4 Strain the gin through a double layer of scalded muslin, then pour into the reserved bottle, seal, and label. Leave the gin to mature, again in a cool, dark place, for as long as you are able: 1 year is good; 3 years even better.

INGREDIENTS

500g (1lb 2oz) frozen sloes

1 x 75cl (1¼ pints) bottle gin

100g (3½oz) white granulated sugar

I always thought it a waste to throw away the sloes used in the sloe gin recipe on p159, so now I reserve them to make this tangy jelly, which I like to serve with roasted game birds.

Sloe gin and juniper jelly

 TAKES 1¼ HOURS   MAKES 1.25KG (2¾LB)   KEEPS FOR 6–9 MONTHS

1   Put the sloes and 500ml (16fl oz) water in a preserving pan, bring to the boil, cover, and simmer for about 1 hour until the sloes are very soft. Spoon into a jelly bag and allow to drip overnight.

2   Put the resulting juice and the correct quantities of lemon juice, sugar, and pectin in the cleaned preserving pan. Bring to the boil, then cook at a full rolling boil for 4 minutes, stirring frequently. Test the mixture for a set.

3   When the jelly has reached setting point, skim off any scum from the surface and add the juniper berries to the jelly. Boil for a further minute, then pot into hot sterilized jars, seal, and label.

INGREDIENTS

500g (1lb 2oz) sloes

10 juniper berries, crushed

FOR EACH 600ML (1 PINT) JUICE

freshly squeezed juice of 1 lemon

500g (1lb 2oz) white granulated sugar

125g (4½oz) liquid pectin

I first tasted this delicious jelly in Galway, Ireland. It's as good spooned onto your morning toast as it is eaten with roast lamb or venison, and is perfect with toasted goat's cheese.

Rowan jelly

 TAKES 40 MINUTES   MAKES 2KG (4½LB)   KEEPS FOR 6–9 MONTHS

1   Put all the fruit in a large preserving pan, and barely cover with water. Bring to the boil, then simmer for 20 minutes or until the fruit is soft. Allow to drip through a jelly bag overnight.

2   Measure the juice and weigh out the correct quantity of sugar. Add the juice and sugar to the cleaned preserving pan, and simmer over a low heat for 10 minutes until the sugar has dissolved.

3   Increase the heat and cook at a full rolling boil for 5 minutes, then test for a set. When the jelly has reached setting point, pot into hot sterilized jars, seal, and label.

INGREDIENTS

1.8kg (4lb) rowan berries, washed, and stalks removed

1.35kg (3lb) cooking apples, peeled, cored, and quartered, or crab apples, peeled and cored

450g (1lb) white granulated sugar for each 600ml (1 pint) juice

Horseradish grows wild in meadows and along roadsides, and is easily recognizable once you know what to look for. It's the root that is used, and it's hottest when freshly prepared.

Horseradish in vinegar

 NO COOKING   MAKES 450G (1LB)   KEEPS FOR 6 WEEKS

1   Grate the horseradish. Take care when doing this, as the root will give off fiery fumes. I recommend using the fine grating blade of a food processor.

2   In a large bowl, sprinkle the salt over the horseradish and leave for 1 hour. Rinse gently under cold running water, then squeeze dry using a clean tea towel. Pack into hot sterilized jars.

3   In a stainless-steel or enamelled saucepan, heat the vinegar to boiling point, then pour over the horseradish to cover it completely. Cover the jars with vinegar-proof seals, label, and store in the refrigerator.

INGREDIENTS

450g (1lb) horseradish root, well scrubbed and peeled

30g (1oz) salt

300ml (10fl oz) white wine vinegar

Do make sure when collecting samphire from the wild that you are not picking in a restricted area. Once you get home, wash it really thoroughly to remove all traces of sand and mud.

Pickled samphire

 NO COOKING   MAKES 450G (1LB)   KEEPS FOR 6 MONTHS

1   Arrange the samphire in layers in a deep bowl, scattering the salt between the layers. Leave for 48 hours, to draw out excess moisture. Rinse thoroughly under cold running water, then pat dry using clean tea towels.

2   Meanwhile, put the vinegar in a stainless-steel or enamelled saucepan, and bring to the boil. Transfer to a clean bowl, add the spices, and leave to infuse for 24–48 hours.

3   Pack the samphire into hot sterilized jars. Pour the spiced vinegar into the cleaned saucepan, bring to boiling point, then pour into the jars. Ensure that the samphire is completely immersed. Cover with vinegar-proof seals, label, and leave to mature for at least 2 weeks.

INGREDIENTS

350g (12oz) fresh samphire, washed

30g (1oz) salt

900ml (1½ pints) distilled malt vinegar, plus extra if needed

1 tbsp crushed coriander seeds

1 tbsp crushed fennel seeds

1 tbsp crushed white peppercorns

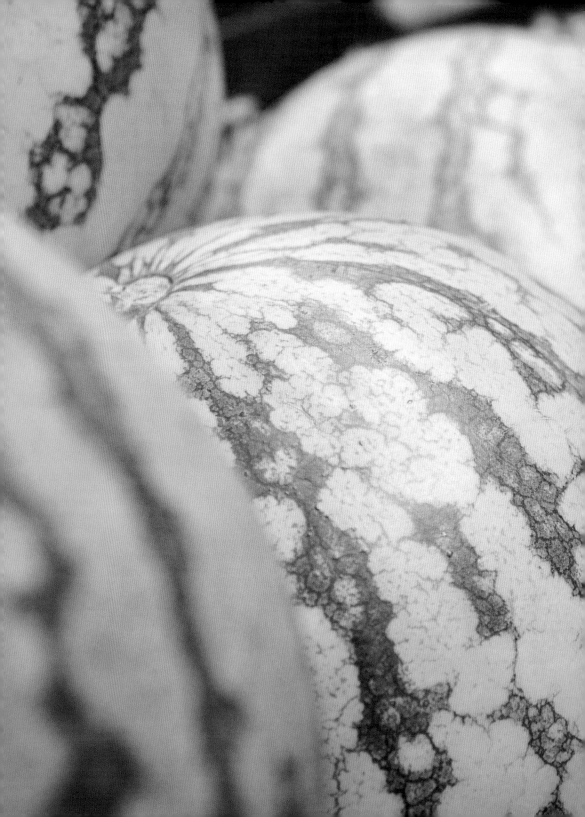

Tropical fruit

Bananas • Kiwi fruit • Mangoes
Melons • Passion fruit • Pineapple
Pomegranate • Watermelon

Use ripe, highly scented melons for this conserve. The usual pairing is to add ginger to the jam, but I like the more subtle notes of vanilla – or, for a real buzz, try some crushed star anise. Serve as a sweetmeat with langues-de-chat biscuits, or as an accompaniment to ice cream.

Melon and vanilla conserve

 TAKES 30 MINUTES   MAKES 1.35KG (3LB)   KEEPS FOR 6–9 MONTHS

1   Arrange the melon in layers in a large china or glass bowl, sprinkling each layer with sugar and squeezing over the lemon juice. Allow to stand for 24 hours to draw out the water from the fruit.

2   Strain the collected liquid into a preserving pan, reserving the melon cubes. Boil rapidly for 15–20 minutes to reduce the liquid by half.

3   Add the melon cubes, and simmer for a further 4–5 minutes to cook the fruit.

4   Stir in the pectin, increase the heat, and cook at a full rolling boil for 2 minutes, then test for a set.

5   When the conserve has reached setting point, skim off any scum from the surface, then stir in the vanilla seeds or crushed star anise. Leave for 5 minutes to allow the jelly to thicken a little, to prevent the melon cubes sinking to the bottom when the conserve is in the jars. Pot into hot sterilized jars, seal, and label.

INGREDIENTS

1.5kg (3lb 3oz) melon flesh, chopped into 2cm (¾in) cubes

1kg (2¼lb) white granulated sugar

freshly squeezed juice of 3 lemons

125g (4½oz) liquid pectin

1 tsp vanilla seeds or 2 star anise, crushed

CHOOSING YOUR MELON

Any variety of melon works well in this recipe, with the exception of watermelon. It is important, though, to choose melon that is ripe, scented, and flavourful. I sometimes add some finely chopped pistachio nuts to give the finished conserve a little texture.

Tropically scented and like sunshine in colour, this preserve is the perfect way to cheer up a dull winter's day. Serve with hot, crusty rolls and fresh coffee for a leisurely weekend breakfast.

Mango, passion fruit, and lime preserve

TAKES 30 MINUTES   MAKES 1.6KG (3½LB)   KEEPS FOR 6 MONTHS

1   Using a teaspoon, scoop the pulp from the passion fruit. Put in a preserving pan with the mango flesh and lime juice. Add 500ml (16fl oz) water, bring the mixture to the boil, and simmer for 20 minutes, or until the fruit is very soft.

2   Add the sugar, stirring until it has dissolved, then cook at a full rolling boil for 3–4 minutes, skimming off any scum that rises to the surface. This preserve produces a lot of scum, so you will need to skim regularly.

3   Stir in the pectin and continue to boil the mixture for 2 minutes, then test for a set.

4   When the conserve has reached setting point, stir in the lime zest. Allow the conserve to settle for 5 minutes, then pot into hot sterilized jars, seal, and label.

VARIATION
No limes to hand? Lemons or even blood oranges make a deliciously different preserve, with no sacrifice of flavour.

INGREDIENTS

8 large ripe passion fruit

4 large ripe mangoes, about 1.1kg (2½lb) total weight, peeled and roughly chopped

finely grated zest and freshly squeezed juice of 4 large limes

750g (1lb 10oz) white granulated sugar

125g (4½oz) liquid pectin

Rather an unusual spread for your morning toast, this is also delicious spooned onto vanilla ice cream or natural yogurt, its fruity and slightly fiery flavour providing the perfect contrast.

Mango and chilli jam

🕐 TAKES 20 MINUTES   🥘 MAKES 1.5KG (3LB 3OZ)   🗄 KEEPS FOR 6 MONTHS

1 Put the mango flesh in a food processor with the chillies, and reduce to a purée. Transfer the mixture to a preserving pan. Add 250ml (8fl oz) water, the sugar, and the lime juice.

2 Heat slowly for about 10 minutes, stirring to dissolve the sugar. Increase the heat and cook at a full rolling boil for 5 minutes.

3 Stir in the pectin. Return to the boil for 2 minutes, then test for a set. When setting point has been reached, pot the jam into hot sterilized jars, seal, and label.

INGREDIENTS

flesh from 4 ripe mangoes, about 750g (1lb 10oz)

3 red chillies, deseeded

650g (1lb 7oz) white granulated sugar

freshly squeezed juice of 3 limes

250g (9oz) liquid pectin

Sadly, these lovely vitamin-packed fruit lose some of their wonderful emerald colour when cooked. Kiwi jam is excellent on buttered scones, or used as a filling for sponge cake.

Kiwi fruit jam

🕐 TAKES 10 MINUTES   🥘 MAKES 1.25KG (2¾LB)   🗄 KEEPS FOR 6 MONTHS

1 Cut out the hard cores of the fruit from the stem end. Put the kiwi fruit and apple juice in a food processor or blender, and blitz until you have a smooth purée. I leave the blacks seeds in, but you can sieve them out if you prefer.

2 Pour the purée into a preserving pan, and stir in the sugar. Warm over a low heat for 5–8 minutes, stirring until the sugar has dissolved. Increase the heat and cook at a full rolling boil for 2 minutes.

3 Turn off the heat and stir in the pectin. Bring the mixture back to the boil, and cook at a full rolling boil for 1 minute, then test for a set.

4 When setting point has been reached, pot the jam into hot sterilized jars, seal, and label.

INGREDIENTS

750g (1lb 10oz) kiwi fruit, peeled

250ml (8fl oz) apple juice

600g (1lb 5oz) white granulated sugar

125g (4½oz) liquid pectin

Preserving tropical fruit

WHAT TO LOOK FOR

Heady with scent but often soft in texture, tropical fruits make wonderful jams and jellies, and marry particularly well with chillies for relishes and chutneys. Each fruit must be checked carefully for ripeness, as many will have travelled some distance to market. Scent is often a good guide, as it is this perfume that you wish to capture in your preserve. Make sure there are no obvious blemishes and, cradling the fruit carefully in your hand, check that the flesh just yields to the touch.

MELONS Cradle the melon gently in your hands and press the stem end. It should yield slightly. Now take a good sniff – ripe fruit should also have a distinctive perfume.

WATERMELON These should be chosen by weight – they should feel heavy. Also, check how perfect the rind is, as this is that part used in preserves.

MANGO Most varieties of mango are excellent for preserving. Larger fruit will yield more flesh, so look for these varieties. Choose unbruised, scented fruit with flesh that yields slightly.

PINEAPPLE The best test for ripeness here is to gently tug a leaf or two in the centre of the crown. If they pull out easily, the pineapple is ripe. If not, it may be too green to use.

PASSION FRUIT As these are encased in a hard shell, testing for ripeness here is not by aroma or softness. Instead, you must look for a somewhat wrinkled skin, but without any mould.

KIWI FRUIT Choose large, unwrinkled fruit that yield a little when squeezed.

This lovely golden conserve makes a special breakfast treat, spread over hot buttered wholemeal toast. Cardamom's warm fragrance has a special affinity with tropical fruit and gives a flavourful lift to the pineapple and apple base of this conserve.

Cardamom and pineapple conserve

🕐 TAKES 30 MINUTES   🍲 MAKES 1.25KG (2¾LB)   🗄 KEEPS FOR 6 MONTHS

1 Chop the pineapple flesh. I whiz mine in a food processor until it is well chopped, stopping just short of a purée. Alternatively, chop it finely using a sharp knife and a chopping board.

2 Put the pineapple and the chopped apples in a preserving pan with the sugar, cardamom seeds, lemon juice, and 150ml (5fl oz) water. Simmer over a gentle heat for 10 minutes, stirring frequently, until all the sugar has dissolved.

3 Increase the heat and cook at a full rolling boil for about 20 minutes, stirring often, until the fruit is cooked and the conserve is thick. Test the mixture for a set.

4 When the conserve has reached setting point, pot into hot sterilized jars, seal, and label.

INGREDIENTS

flesh of 2 ripe medium pineapples, about 750g (1lb 10oz)

500g (1lb 2oz) cooking apples, peeled, cored, and chopped

750g (1lb 10oz) white granulated sugar

1 tsp cardamom seeds, crushed

freshly squeezed juice of 2 large lemons

VARIATION
For a change of flavour, add about 2 tablespoons freshly grated root ginger along with the other ingredients.

Passion fruit have a wonderful but elusive flavour. Make this jelly in small batches and serve with scones, and on sweet breads such as brioche.

Passion fruit jelly

🕐 TAKES 8 MINUTES   🍲 MAKES 675G (1½LB)   🥫 KEEPS FOR 6 MONTHS

1   Scoop the pulp from 10 of the passion fruit, and put the pulp into a preserving pan with the apple juice. Bring to the boil and simmer for 5 minutes. Spoon into a jelly bag and allow to drip overnight.

2   Measure the juice: you should have about 500ml (16fl oz). Weigh out the correct quantity of sugar and add to the cleaned pan with the juice. Stir over a low heat until the sugar has dissolved. Bring to the boil, then simmer for 2 minutes, skimming off any scum.

3   Turn off the heat and add the pulp from the remaining passion fruit. Stir well, increase the heat, and cook at a full rolling boil for about 1 minute. Test for a set.

4   When the jelly has reached setting point, allow to cool for 5 minutes before potting into hot sterilized jars. Seal and label.

INGREDIENTS

12 large ripe passion fruit

500ml (16fl oz) fresh apple juice

100g (3½oz) white granulated sugar for each 100ml (3½fl oz) juice

---

This very simple jelly ticks all the boxes by providing a wonderful jewel-like preserve combined with absolute simplicity of preparation – a combination that's hard to resist.

Pomegranate jelly

🕐 TAKES 5 MINUTES   🍲 MAKES 2KG (4½LB)   🥫 KEEPS FOR 6–9 MONTHS

1   Put all the ingredients in a preserving pan, and bring the mixture slowly to the boil.

2   When the sugar has dissolved, cook the mixture at a full rolling boil for 2 minutes, then test for a set.

3   Once setting point has been reached, pot the jelly into hot sterilized jars, seal, and label.

INGREDIENTS

1 litre (1¾ pints) best-quality pomegranate juice

1kg (2¼lb) white granulated sugar

125g (4½oz) liquid pectin

freshly squeezed juice of 2 lemons

A sweet relish with a touch of chilli, this is excellent with grilled chicken and firm fish such as tuna and swordfish. To tell whether a pineapple is ripe, try lifting it holding only one of the leaves in the middle of the crown – the leaf should pull easily from the fruit.

Pineapple and red onion relish

🕐 TAKES 35 MINUTES   🍲 MAKES 1KG (2¼LB)   🥫 KEEPS FOR 6–9 MONTHS

1   Using a sharp knife, cut the pineapple into wedges, removing the hard central core. Chop the flesh coarsely.

2   Put all the ingredients into a large preserving pan, and bring slowly to the boil, stirring often to ensure that the sugar dissolves.

3   Simmer the relish over a medium heat for 25 minutes until the mixture thickens. To test whether the relish is ready, drag a wooden spoon through the mixture at the bottom of the pan. It should leave a clear channel (see p22).

4   Pot the pineapple relish into hot sterilized jars, cover the jars with vinegar-proof seals, and label.

INGREDIENTS

flesh of 1 large or 2 ripe medium pineapples, 750g (1lb 10oz)

3 large red onions, chopped

2–6 red chillies, deseeded if liked, and chopped

4 plump garlic cloves, crushed

2 tbsp fresh thyme leaves

300g (10oz) white granulated sugar

360ml (12fl oz) white wine vinegar

1 tsp salt

PAIRING FOR COLOUR AND FLAVOUR

I love the colour red onions give this relish, but shallots also work well if you are willing to forgo the distinctive hue the onions impart – and you will not be sacrificing any of the flavour. You will need about 500g (1lb 2oz) peeled and chopped shallots in place of the onion.

This lovely preserve is delicious with hot buttered toast or muffins. Economical, too, it uses the usually discarded white watermelon rind, between the pink flesh and the green outer skin. Although a little fiddly to prepare, it needs no great skill – just patience, and a sharp knife.

Sweet watermelon preserve

🕐 TAKES 2 HOURS 🍲 MAKES 600G (1LB 5OZ) 🗄 KEEPS FOR 6–9 MONTHS

1 Using a small, sharp knife, cut the rind into strips about 1cm (½in) wide and about 2.5cm (1in) long.

2 To make the brine, put the salt and 500ml (16fl oz) water in a large china or glass bowl, stirring to dissolve the salt. Add the watermelon rind and leave, covered, in a cool place for 24 hours.

3 Rinse the rind well under cold running water, and drain.

4 For the syrup, put the sugar and 1 litre (1¾ pints) water in a large preserving pan. Add the lemon rind. Bring the mixture to the boil, and add the drained watermelon rind. Simmer, partially covered, over the lowest possible heat for 1–2 hours until the rind is cooked through and translucent. Check on the pan occasionally to ensure that there is still some liquid in the pan; if not, add extra water.

5 Once the rind is tender and translucent, remove and discard the lemon peel, and spoon the rind carefully into hot sterilized jars. Spoon the syrup over the top.

6 Seal the jars, label, and store in a cool, dark place until needed.

VARIATION
You can use other citrus fruit instead of the lemon in this recipe. Both orange and lime work well, providing that distinctive citrus tang.

INGREDIENTS

600g (1lb 5oz) white watermelon rind from 1 largish melon, green outer skin removed

60g (2oz) table salt

FOR THE SYRUP

600g (1lb 5oz) white granulated sugar

2 or 3 strips of lemon rind

Pickling watermelon rind is a clever way of using up the enormous amount of rind per melon that would otherwise be discarded. Although the recipe takes several days to complete, once the rind is prepared the rest is simplicity. Serve with cold meats, cheeses, and sandwiches.

Watermelon rind pickle

⏱ TAKES 40–60 MINUTES   🍲 MAKES 600G (ILB 5OZ)   🥫 KEEPS FOR UP TO I YEAR

1　Using a small, sharp knife, cut the rind into strips about 1cm (½in) wide and about 2.5cm (1in) long.

2　To make the brine, put the salt and 500ml (16fl oz) water in a large china, glass, or earthenware bowl, stirring to dissolve the salt. Add the rind and leave, covered, in the refrigerator for 3 days.

3　Rinse the rind well under cold running water, and drain.

4　To make the pickling liquid, put the vinegar, 1 litre (1¾ pints) water, sugar, and spices in a large stainless-steel or enamelled saucepan. Bring the mixture to the boil, and add the watermelon rind.

5　Simmer the rind in the liquid for 40–60 minutes until the rind is cooked through and translucent. You may need to add more water as the mixture reduces.

6　Once the rind is tender, pack it into hot sterilized jars. Spoon over the pickling liquid and spices. Cover the jars with vinegar-proof seals, label, and store in a cool, dark place.

VARIATION

I love this combination of spices, but you can vary them to suit your taste, perhaps adding fresh root ginger or even chopped fresh red chilli.

INGREDIENTS

600g (1lb 5oz) white watermelon rind from 1 largish melon, peeled

60g (2oz) table salt

FOR THE PICKLING LIQUID

500ml (16fl oz) cider vinegar

250g (9oz) light muscovado sugar

10cm (4in) cinnamon stick, roughly crushed

6 cloves, roughly crushed

6 allspice berries, about ½ tsp, roughly crushed

Use whatever combination of dried fruit suits your taste, but try to make it as varied as possible. This recipe takes very little time to cook. The high proportion of dried fruit helps it to thicken quickly. Serve with crackers or crusty bread, and firm mature cheese such as Cheddar.

Mango chutney

🕐 TAKES 30 MINUTES   🍲 MAKES ABOUT 2KG (4½LB)   🥫 KEEPS FOR UP TO 1 YEAR

1 Cut any of the larger dried fruit such as apricots, dates, or peaches into 1cm (½in) pieces.

2 Transfer all of the dried fruit to a large heavy preserving pan, and stir in the remaining ingredients.

3 Bring the mixture to the boil, then reduce the heat and simmer for 30 minutes or until the chutney is thick, stirring occasionally to prevent it catching on the bottom of the pan.

4 While the chutney is still hot, pot into hot sterilized jars, cover the jars with vinegar-proof lids, and label.

INGREDIENTS

675g (1½lb) mixed dried fruit (such as apricots, figs, dates, peaches, raisins)

1.35kg (3lb) mangoes, chopped

675g (1½lb) light muscovado sugar

2 large onions, chopped

6 plump garlic cloves, chopped

60g (2oz) fresh root ginger, peeled and grated

1–2 dried red chillies, crushed

1 tbsp salt

1 litre cider or distilled malt vinegar

Side dishes of sliced bananas can be served with curries, but this relish is a little more sophisticated. It is good with chicken and seafood curries, as well as with roast poultry and warm goat's cheese salads.

Fresh banana relish

 TAKES 20 MINUTES  MAKES 900G (2LB) KEEPS FOR 3 MONTHS

1 Heat the oil in a large heavy pan over a medium heat, and sweat the onion for a few minutes until soft and translucent. Add the garlic and ginger, and sweat for a further 1–2 minutes until the onion is soft but still not coloured.

2 Add the cumin seeds and whole dried chillies, and fry for a few minutes to release their flavour. Now add the orange zest, raisins, vinegar, and sugar, and bring the mixture to simmering point.

3 Peel and thinly slice the bananas, and add these to the pan along with the salt. Simmer the mixture for 7–10 minutes until thick.

4 Pot the relish into hot sterilized jars, cover the jars with vinegar-proof seals, and label. Store in the refrigerator.

VARIATION
For a delightful variation on this recipe, add 60g (2oz) desiccated coconut at the same time as the bananas and salt.

INGREDIENTS

2 tbsp vegetable oil

1 medium onion, finely chopped

1 plump garlic clove, crushed

2.5cm (1in) piece of fresh root ginger, finely grated

1 tsp whole cumin seeds, crushed

3–4 dried red chillies

finely grated zest of 1 orange

60g (2 oz) seedless raisins

120ml (4fl oz) white wine vinegar

115g (4oz) light muscovado sugar

450g (1lb) slightly green bananas

1/2 tsp salt

Home-made fruit liqueurs provide a delicious end to a meal. I make several varieties so that I can offer friends a choice. They are all quite sweet and therefore work well when stored in the freezer or served 'on the rocks'. They are also delicious in syllabubs and poured over ice cream.

Passion fruit gin

🕐 NO COOKING   🍲 MAKES 75CL (1¼ PINTS)   🫙 KEEPS FOR UP TO 18 MONTHS

1   Scrape the pulp from the passion fruit into a clean glass bowl. Now stir in the gin and sugar. (Keep the gin bottle for later use.) Cover the bowl with a double layer of cling film. Transfer to a cool, dark place.

2   Over the next 3–4 days, stir the liqueur occasionally until the sugar dissolves, then leave for 4 weeks before straining into the reserved gin bottle. Store either in a cool, dark place, or in the freezer.

INGREDIENTS

8 large ripe passion fruit

75cl (1¼ pints) gin (40% proof if possible)

250g (9oz) white granulated sugar

This delightful cordial dates from Tudor times and makes a refreshing summer drink and a spicy addition to a white wine punch – it couldn't be easier to make.

Hypocras

🕐 TAKES 7 MINUTES   🍲 MAKES 600ML (1 PINT)   🫙 KEEPS FOR 6 MONTHS

1   Make a sugar syrup. Dissolve the sugar in 600ml (1 pint) water in a saucepan, and bring the liquid to the boil. Simmer for 5 minutes. Add the cinnamon, cardamom, and ginger, then cover the pan and leave to stand for 24 hours.

2   Strain the syrup through scalded muslin into hot sterilized bottles, seal, and label. Store in a cool, dark place.

INGREDIENTS

225g (8oz) white granulated sugar

10cm (4in) cinnamon stick, broken into pieces

2 tsp cardamom pods, crushed

5cm (2in) piece of fresh root ginger, crushed

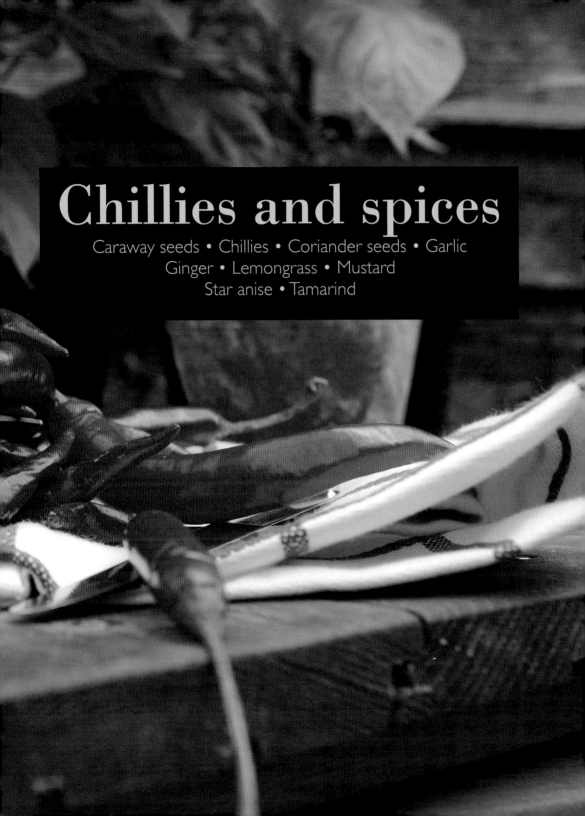

Chillies and spices

Caraway seeds • Chillies • Coriander seeds • Garlic
Ginger • Lemongrass • Mustard
Star anise • Tamarind

Hailing from Louisiana, this vibrant jelly is eaten with crackers and cream cheese. For extra bite, the chillies in this recipe retain their seeds, but they may be deseeded if preferred.

Red pepper jelly

🕐 TAKES 10 MINUTES   🍲 MAKES 1.5KG (3½LB)   🫙 KEEPS FOR 6 MONTHS

1   Put the peppers and chillies in a blender or food processor, and chop finely. Alternatively, chop by hand.

2   Transfer the chopped peppers and chillies to a deep heavy saucepan. Add the vinegar, and bring to the boil. Boil for 5 minutes, then allow to drip through a jelly bag overnight.

3   Pour the resulting liquid into a large saucepan, and add the sugar. Bring the mixture slowly to the boil over a medium heat, stirring until the sugar has dissolved.

4   Add the pectin, increase the heat, and cook at a full rolling boil for 2 minutes, then test for a set.

5   When the jelly has reached setting point, pot into small sterilized jars, and cover with vinegar-proof seals. Do label the jars carefully, as you wouldn't want to spread this jelly on your morning toast!

INGREDIENTS

6 large red peppers, stalks removed, halved, and deseeded

12 red chillies, halved

600ml (1 pint) red wine vinegar

1.25kg (2¾lb) white granulated sugar

250g (9oz) liquid pectin

CHOOSING YOUR CHILLIES

The version of this fiery jelly given here uses fresh red chillies, but you can use dried red chillies if you don't have fresh ones to hand. Simply soak the dried chillies in water overnight, then drain and proceed with the recipe as above.

Perfect for the garlic lover, this jelly is fabulous with lamb and pork dishes. I also like to serve it with toasted goat's cheese and young rocket leaves.

Garlic and green chilli jelly

🕐 TAKES 50 MINUTES　　 MAKES 1.7KG (1¾LB)　　 KEEPS FOR 6 MONTHS

1　Using a food processor or blender, whiz the garlic and chillies to a paste. There is no need to peel the garlic or deseed the chillies. Alternatively, pound to a paste with a mortar and pestle.

2　Transfer the paste to a preserving pan with the apples and 1 litre (1¾ pints) water. Bring the mixture to the boil. Cover and simmer for about 40 minutes until all the ingredients are very soft. Spoon the mixture into a jelly bag, and allow to drip overnight.

3　Put the resulting liquid, vinegar, salt, and sugar in a clean preserving pan. Stir over a low heat to dissolve the sugar, then cook at a full rolling boil for 5 minutes, or until setting point has been reached. Pot into hot sterilized jars, cover with vinegar-proof seals, and label.

INGREDIENTS

2 heads of fresh garlic

6–8 green chillies

1kg (2¼lb) cooking apples, roughly chopped

2 tbsp white wine vinegar

1 tsp salt

450g (1lb) white granulated sugar

Another pretty apple-based jelly, this one is flecked with pieces of lemongrass and red chilli.

Lemongrass and chilli jelly

🕐 TAKES 40 MINUTES　　 MAKES 1.5KG (3½LB)　　 KEEPS FOR 6 MONTHS

1　Chop the apples and 2 of the chillies. Put the apples, chopped chilli, 3 lemongrass stalks, and 1.5 litres (2¾ pints) water in a preserving pan. Simmer for 30 minutes until the apples are very soft. Spoon the mixture into a jelly bag, and leave to drip overnight.

2　Measure the resulting juice, and weigh out the correct quantity of sugar. Put in a preserving pan, and stir over a low heat until the sugar has dissolved. Increase the heat and cook at a full rolling boil for 5 minutes until setting point has been reached.

3　Chop the extra length of lemongrass and remaining chillies. Add both to the jelly, and boil for a further minute. Allow the jelly to cool for 5 minutes, then pot into small sterilized jars, seal, and label.

INGREDIENTS

1.5kg (3lb 3oz) cooking apples

5 large red chillies, deseeded

3 lemongrass stalks, crushed, plus extra 4cm (1½in) length

500g (1lb 2oz) white granulated sugar for each 500ml (16fl oz) juice

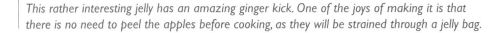

This rather interesting jelly has an amazing ginger kick. One of the joys of making it is that there is no need to peel the apples before cooking, as they will be strained through a jelly bag.

Ginger jelly

🕐 TAKES 50 MINUTES   🍲 MAKES 2KG (4½LB)   🥫 KEEPS FOR 6 MONTHS

1 Chop the apples and put in a preserving pan with 1 litre (1¾ pints) water and the ginger, and bring to the boil. Cover and simmer for 30 minutes until the fruit is pulpy. Spoon the apple mixture into a jelly bag, and allow to drip for 6 hours or overnight.

2 Measure the resulting juice, and weigh out the correct quantity of sugar. Gently simmer the juice and sugar in the cleaned preserving pan, stirring until the sugar has dissolved. Increase the heat and cook at a full rolling boil for 10 minutes until setting point is reached.

3 Skim off any scum, and stir in the preserved ginger and ginger wine, if using. Return to the boil, then turn off the heat and leave to stand for 10 minutes to allow the jelly to thicken slightly (so that the ginger pieces do not sink). Pot into hot sterilized jars, seal, and label.

INGREDIENTS

2kg (4½lb) cooking apples

200g (7oz) fresh root ginger, finely chopped

500g (1lb 2oz) white granulated sugar for each 600ml (1 pint) juice

5 or 6 pieces of preserved stem ginger, finely chopped

60ml (2fl oz) ginger wine (optional)

Spiked with sweet Spanish smoked paprika, this jam goes well with cheeses or cold meats.

Red pepper and chilli jam

🕐 TAKES 15 MINUTES   🍲 MAKES 1KG (2¼LB)   🥫 KEEPS FOR 6 MONTHS

1 Remove the stalks from the red peppers and chillies, then halve and deseed. Transfer to a blender or food processor, and chop finely. Alternatively, chop with a sharp knife.

2 Transfer to a deep heavy saucepan, and add the vinegar and sugar. Bring the mixture slowly to the boil, stirring until the sugar has dissolved. Boil rapidly for 5 minutes. Turn off the heat, and stir in the pectin. Add the pimenton dulce.

3 Turn on the heat and cook at a full rolling boil for 2 minutes, then test for a set. When the jam has reached setting point, allow it to settle for 5 minutes, then pot into hot sterilized jars, seal, and label.

INGREDIENTS

5 large red peppers

4–8 red chillies

360ml (12fl oz) white wine vinegar

1.25kg (2¾lb) white granulated sugar

125g (4oz) liquid pectin

2 tbsp pimenton dulce (sweet smoked paprika)

Preserving with peppers

HOW TO USE PEPPERS

All peppers, both sweet and hot, belong to the Capsicum genus, which is part of the Solanaceae family that includes tomatoes, potatoes, and aubergines – as well as tobacco, the flowering plant datura, and deadly nightshade. Hot chilli peppers are used to add a fiery flavour to food. This heat comes from the chemical capsaicin, which is concentrated in the pith. Removing the pith along with the seeds reduces the heat, while still allowing a good, full flavour.

Grading by heat

On the Scoville Scale, developed by Wilbur Scoville in 1912, peppers are graded as to the heat they impart, with chilli peppers at one end of the scale and sweet peppers at the other. If you are not sure how hot a pepper is, use a small quantity – it is easier to add heat than take it out. Also remember that different chillies of the same variety can vary in capsaicin content. Green peppers and chillies are simply unripe red, yellow, or orange ones, and have a fresher flavour. Green chillies are milder than hot ones, as capsaicin develops with ripeness: choose plump, unwrinkled ones for cooking. Red chillies can be used at all stages of ripeness and freshness. The riper and dryer the chillies are, the more concentrated the flavour.

- **Hot peppers** include habañero, Scotch bonnet, cayenne, and serrano chillies.
- **Medium peppers** include jalapeño, chipotle, and poblano.
- **Mild peppers** include bell or sweet peppers.

Hot peppers

SERRANO chillies are very hot and are available either fresh or dried.

SCOTCH BONNET chillies are among the hottest in the world, and should be used with care.

BIRD'S-EYE chillies are very high in capsaicin and have a good flavour.

INDIAN HOT chillies are the best choice for curries and vindaloo spice pastes.

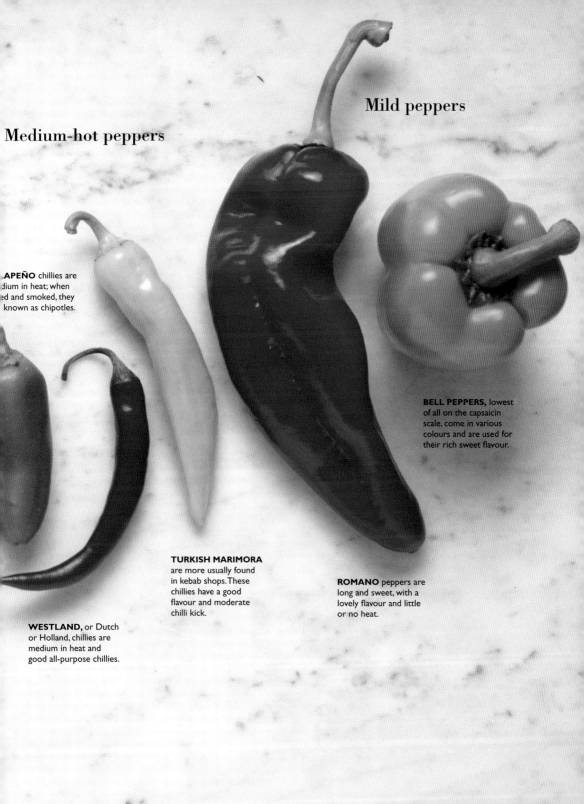

Medium-hot peppers

Mild peppers

APEÑO chillies are
dium in heat; when
ed and smoked, they
known as chipotles.

BELL PEPPERS, lowest
of all on the capsaicin
scale, come in various
colours and are used for
their rich sweet flavour.

TURKISH MARIMORA
are more usually found
in kebab shops. These
chillies have a good
flavour and moderate
chilli kick.

ROMANO peppers are
long and sweet, with a
lovely flavour and little
or no heat.

WESTLAND, or Dutch
or Holland, chillies are
medium in heat and
good all-purpose chillies.

This lovely tangy chutney uses tamarind paste, available from good supermarkets or specialist food stores, to add sharpness to the sweet tomatoes, while celery seeds provide the base note.

Tomato and tamarind chutney

🕐 TAKES 35 MINUTES   🍲 MAKES 1.6KG (3½LB)   🥫 KEEPS FOR 9 MONTHS

1   Put all the ingredients in a large preserving pan, and bring the mixture slowly to the boil. Simmer for 20–30 minutes, stirring often, then test that the chutney is thick enough. It will take longer to cook if the tomatoes are very juicy.

2   When the chutney has reached the desired consistency, pot into hot sterilized jars, cover the jars with vinegar-proof seals, and label.

VARIATION
You can replace the celery seed used in this chutney with crushed cardamom seeds, and add some finely grated orange zest, too.

INGREDIENTS

1kg (2¼lb) tomatoes, roughly chopped

4 large onions, finely chopped

150g (5½oz) celery, finely chopped

4 red chillies, deseeded if liked, and chopped

6 plump garlic cloves, crushed

150g (5½oz) sultanas

2 tbsp tamarind paste

1 tsp celery seed

300g (10oz) golden granulated sugar

1 tbsp salt

400ml (14fl oz) cider vinegar

This spice mix comes from North Africa, where it is commonly rubbed onto fish. I also like it to use it on white meats such as pork and chicken. It makes a tasty marinade for tofu, too.

Chermoula

🕐 TAKES 5 MINUTES   🥣 MAKES 300G (10OZ)   🫙 KEEPS FOR 4 WEEKS

1   Crush the garlic. Grind the cumin and coriander seeds in a spice mill or coffee grinder, or use a mortar and pestle.

2   Put all the ingredients in a small saucepan. Add 120ml (4fl oz) water, and bring to the boil. Simmer for 4–5 minutes until reduced by half.

3   Pour the mixture into a hot, sterilized jar, cover with a vinegar-proof seal, and label. Store in the refrigerator until needed.

INGREDIENTS

4 garlic cloves

3 tsp cumin seeds

4 tbsp coriander seeds

2 tbsp pimenton dulce (sweet smoked paprika)

1 tsp cayenne pepper

100ml (3½fl oz) red wine vinegar

freshly squeezed juice of 3 lemons

150ml (5fl oz) olive oil

Found throughout North Africa, this fiery sauce should be used in small doses! A traditional accompaniment to tagines, it can also spice up anything from casseroles to cornbreads.

Harissa

🕐 NO COOKING   🥣 MAKES 115G (4OZ)   🫙 KEEPS FOR 4 MONTHS

1   Soak the chillies in water for 30 minutes, then drain.

2   Whiz the chillies in a food processor or blender with the garlic, spices, and enough of the 4 tbsp olive oil to make a soft paste. Alternatively, pound the chillies, garlic, spices, and salt to a paste using a mortar and pestle, then add the oil.

3   Press into a hot sterilized jar, cover with extra oil, seal, and label. Store the harissa in the refrigerator.

INGREDIENTS

60g (2oz) dried red chillies

4 garlic cloves

1 tsp caraway seeds

1 tsp coriander seeds

½ tsp salt

4 tbsp olive oil, plus extra to cover

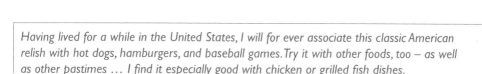

Having lived for a while in the United States, I will for ever associate this classic American relish with hot dogs, hamburgers, and baseball games. Try it with other foods, too – as well as other pastimes … I find it especially good with chicken or grilled fish dishes.

Corn and chilli relish

 TAKES 40 MINUTES   MAKES 900G (2LB)   KEEPS FOR 6–9 MONTHS

1 Put all the ingredients except the salt in a large preserving pan, and cook the mixture over a low heat, stirring occasionally, until the sugar has dissolved.

2 Bring to the boil, then simmer for 20 minutes until the relish has thickened slightly. Test that it has achieved the right consistency: the relish is ready when there is still a little loose liquid in the pan. As this is a chunky relish, it will be a little wetter than a chutney.

3 Add the salt and stir the chutney until the salt has dissolved.

4 Pot the relish into hot sterilized jars, cover with vinegar-proof seals, and label.

VARIATION
Green peppers and green chillies, being milder in flavour, give a change both to the appearance and to the taste of this relish.

INGREDIENTS

500g (1lb 2oz) corn kernels, cut from 4–5 cobs

2 red chillies, deseeded if liked, and chopped

115g (4oz) deseeded and chopped red pepper

115g (4oz) celery, chopped

115g (4oz) red onion, chopped

175g (6oz) white granulated sugar

freshly squeezed juice of 1 large lemon

300ml (10fl oz) white wine vinegar

1 tsp mustard powder

½ tsp celery seed

2 tbsp salt

This is my favourite barbecue sauce. Remember that it's very sticky-sweet and so has a tendency to burn easily. When using it, baste it onto the food towards the end of cooking.

Smoky barbecue sauce

 TAKES 15 MINUTES   MAKES 750ML (1¼ PINTS)   KEEPS FOR 6 WEEKS

1   Put all the ingredients in a large saucepan, and whisk together until smooth. Bring the mixture slowly to the boil, whisking occasionally, until the sugar is dissolved.

2   Simmer the sauce for 10–15 minutes until it thickens and becomes syrupy.

3   Pour into hot, sterilized bottles, seal with vinegar-proof lids, and label. Store the sauce in the refrigerator.

VARIATION

If you can find liquid smoke in your local delicatessen, add about 1 tablespoon to the mix for a truly smoky flavour. When diluted by 50 per cent with water, this sauce is ideal for oven-baked spare ribs.

INGREDIENTS

600ml (1 pint) orange juice

175g (6oz) light muscovado sugar

200ml (7fl oz) Worcestershire sauce

200ml (7fl oz) dark soy sauce

150ml (5fl oz) cider vinegar

300ml (10fl oz) tomato ketchup

4 garlic cloves, crushed

4 tbsp mild ready-made mustard

Tabasco sauce, to taste

freshly ground black pepper, to taste

This Indonesian take on soy sauce is much more complex than other East and Southeast Asian varieties. It makes an excellent barbecue marinade, and a great addition to stir-fries.

Ketjap manis

 TAKES 15 MINUTES  MAKES 400ML (14FL OZ) 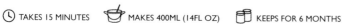 KEEPS FOR 6 MONTHS

1 Put all the ingredients in a heavy saucepan. Place over a low heat and simmer slowly, stirring, until the sugar has dissolved.

2 Increase the heat and continue to simmer for 5 minutes, stirring often until the mixture thickens and becomes syrupy. Remember that it will thicken slightly as it cools.

3 Have ready a sieve, lined with scalded muslin. When the sauce is thickened to your liking, strain it through the sieve, then pot into hot sterilized jars, seal, and label. Store in either a cool, dark place or the refrigerator, until needed.

INGREDIENTS

500ml (16fl oz) dark soy sauce

250g (9oz) light muscovado sugar

250g (9oz) black treacle

4 garlic cloves, crushed

5cm (2in) piece of fresh root ginger, finely chopped

2–3 star anise, crushed

1 tbsp coriander seeds

This sauce is delicious with roast duck, hot dogs, and barbecue dishes. For a more textured sauce, replace the mustard powder with 200g (7oz) coarse-grain prepared mustard.

Orange and honey mustard sauce

TAKES 15 MINUTES  MAKES 600G (1LB 5OZ)  KEEPS FOR 3 MONTHS

1 Put the garlic and salt in a bowl, and mash together until you have a smooth purée. Strip the leaves from the thyme sprigs.

2 Transfer the garlic purée and thyme leaves to a heavy saucepan. Add the remaining ingredients, and bring the mixture to the boil, whisking to blend in the mustard powder.

3 Boil rapidly for about 10 minutes until the sauce reduces and thickens. It should be the consistency of double cream.

4 Pot into hot sterilized jars, cover with vinegar-proof seals, and label. This sauce may separate, so shake the jar before use.

INGREDIENTS

4 garlic cloves

1 tbsp salt

3 sprigs of fresh thyme leaves

juice of 6 oranges

50g (1¾oz) English mustard powder

200ml (7fl oz) cider vinegar

350g (12oz) clear honey

A glut of chillies prompted me to make this dipping sauce for the first time. It's so easy to do and has such a superior flavour to the ready-made version that I always make my own now.

Sweet chilli dipping sauce

🕐 TAKES 10–15 MINUTES   🍲 MAKES 750ML (1¼ PINTS)   🥫 KEEPS FOR 6 MONTHS

1   Put the vinegar and sugar in a large deep saucepan, and bring slowly to the boil, stirring until the sugar has dissolved.

2   Increase the heat and boil rapidly for 5 minutes until the mixture becomes syrupy.

3   Add the chillies and salt, and cook for a further 3–4 minutes. Take care as the mixture will bubble up at first.

4   Pot into hot sterilized jars, cover with vinegar-proof seals, and label.

INGREDIENTS

1 litre (1¾ pints) 5% alcohol rice wine vinegar

850g (1lb 14oz) white granulated sugar

350g (12oz) red chillies, finely chopped but retaining pith and seeds

2 tbsp salt

This Japanese barbecue sauce is delicious with pork, chicken, tofu, or prawns. Mirin is a rice wine and is available from good supermarkets or specialist food stores.

Teriyaki sauce

🕐 TAKES 10 MINUTES   🍲 MAKES 500ML (16FL OZ)   🥫 KEEPS FOR 2 MONTHS

1   Put all the ingredients in a saucepan, and bring slowly to the boil. Once the sugar has dissolved, simmer the sauce for 5 minutes.

2   Pour into a sterilized bottle and seal. Store in the refrigerator.

INGREDIENTS

250ml (8fl oz) dark soy sauce

250ml (8fl oz) mirin

60g (2oz) white granulated sugar

The choice of crunchy or smooth peanut butter for this recipe is a matter of taste – I prefer the rougher texture that the crunchy type gives. Serve with barbecued chicken, pork, or fish.

Chilli, peanut, and garlic sauce

 TAKES 10 MINUTES  MAKES 800G (1¾LB) KEEPS FOR 6 WEEKS

1 Finely chop the garlic. Deseed the chillies if liked, for a milder flavour, then chop.

2 Put all ingredients in a saucepan, and whisk well to combine. Bring to the boil, then simmer for 5 minutes. Be careful as the mixture can plop and bubble, spitting hot sauce onto your hands.

3 When the mixture has thickened to the consistency of thick custard, pot into hot sterilized jars, cover with vinegar-proof seals, and label. Store in the refrigerator.

INGREDIENTS

8 garlic cloves

3–4 large red chillies

250g (9oz) peanut butter

250g (9oz) light muscovado sugar

300ml (10fl oz) red wine vinegar

1 tsp salt

As useful at Christmas as on summer picnics, this is a storecupboard recipe to make year-round. Serve with pâtés, game terrines, or a hard cheese such as mature Cheddar.

Sweet and sour pickled figs

 TAKES 10 MINUTES  MAKES 600G (1LB 5OZ) KEEPS FOR UP TO 1 YEAR

1 Dried figs are sometimes coated in cornflour before being packaged for sale. If yours have been prepared this way, wash them well and allow to drain, then remove the stems and slice finely.

2 Put the figs in a stainless-steel or enamelled pan with the sugar, chillies, and vinegar, and warm gently, stirring until the sugar dissolves.

3 Simmer the mixture gently for 3–5 minutes until the figs begin to soften. If the mixture is very dry, add more vinegar.

4 Allow the pickle to cool a little before potting into hot sterilized jars, covering with vinegar-proof seals, and labelling. Allow the figs to mature for about 4 weeks before using.

INGREDIENTS

500g (1lb 2oz) good-quality dried figs

85g (3oz) dark muscovado sugar

2–3 dried chillies, finely chopped

300ml (10fl oz) red wine vinegar, plus extra if necessary

A wonderful addition to any cook's pantry, these peppers are as beautiful to look at as they are delicious to eat. Serve with antipasti, or slice into salads for extra colour and flavour.

Pickled sweet peppers

⏱ TAKES 30 MINUTES   🍲 MAKES 600G (1LB 5OZ)   🥫 KEEPS FOR 3 MONTHS

1 Roast the peppers under a hot grill or on a barbecue until the skins are blistered and black. Put in a glass or china bowl while hot, cover with cling film, and allow to cool.

2 When cold, peel and deseed the peppers. Finely slice and pack into hot sterilized jars.

3 Meanwhile, combine the vinegar, sugar, chilli flakes, and salt in a saucepan, and bring to the boil. Simmer the mixture for 10 minutes or until reduced by half.

4 Pour the boiling mixture over the peppers, making sure that they are completely submerged, and adding extra vinegar if necessary. Cover with vinegar-proof seals, label, and store in a cool, dark place for up to 6 weeks before using. Once opened, store in the refrigerator.

INGREDIENTS

4 large ripe red peppers

360ml (12fl oz) white wine vinegar, plus extra if necessary

3 tbsp white granulated sugar

good pinch of dried red chilli flakes

1 tsp salt

Rather wicked, but this is just the thing to kickstart a Bloody Mary. Store the vodka in the freezer, and serve in shot glasses or as part of a vibrant cocktail.

Chilli vodka

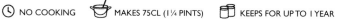

⏱ NO COOKING   🍲 MAKES 75CL (1¼ PINTS)   🥫 KEEPS FOR UP TO 1 YEAR

1 Add the chillies to the vodka. Shake well every day for a week.

2 Transfer the bottle to the freezer and leave until really cold. The vodka is then ready to use.

INGREDIENTS

3–10 red chillies, deseeded if liked, and chopped

1 x 75cl (1¼ pints) bottle vodka

Served in sushi bars worldwide, this pretty pickle works well with fish and chicken dishes. Chopped finely, it can be mixed into Oriental salad dressings, or folded through freshly cooked rice with a touch of wasabi paste, to serve with steamed fish.

Pink pickled ginger

○ TAKES 1¼ HOURS   🍲 MAKES 500G (1LB 2OZ)   🗄 KEEPS FOR 4 MONTHS

1 Peel the ginger if necessary, then slice it finely and put the slices in a large bowl.

2 Sprinkle the ginger with the salt and toss so that it is thoroughly coated. Allow the mixture to sit for 1 hour, then rinse the slices and pat dry using kitchen paper.

3 Pack the ginger into hot sterilized jars.

4 Put the vinegar and sugar in a stainless-steel or enamelled saucepan. Heat gently, stirring until the sugar has dissolved. Bring to the boil, then pour the vinegar over the ginger while still hot.

5 Cover the jars with vinegar-proof seals, label, and allow the pickle to cool before storing in the refrigerator.

INGREDIENTS

500g (1lb 2oz) fresh young root ginger

1 tbsp salt

250ml (8fl oz) rice wine vinegar

115g (4oz) caster sugar

PREPARING THE GINGER

As it matures, the pickled ginger turns a pretty pink. To get this effect, however, you ideally need to use young ginger. You can find this in Oriental markets or specialist food stores. Very young ginger does not need peeling. If it is slightly older, I find the easiest way to remove the skin is to scrape it off with a teaspoon.

Winter citrus

Clementines • Grapefruit • Kumquats
Lemons • Limes
Seville oranges • Sweet oranges

This is a real old-fashioned favourite. If you can find organic Seville oranges and ginger, do use them. This recipe makes a large quantity of marmalade, but it stores well, so will not be wasted.

Orange and ginger marmalade

🕐 TAKES 1½ HOURS   🍲 MAKES 4.4KG (10LB)   🫙 KEEPS FOR UP TO 1 YEAR

1   Wash the oranges under warm running water, then put them, whole, along with the ginger and 2.25 litres (4 pints) water, in a preserving pan. Bring the mixture to the boil. Cover with a lid and simmer for 40–50 minutes until the fruit is soft.

2   Using a slotted spoon, remove the ginger and fruit from the pan, and set aside. Measure the cooking liquid and make this up to 1.7 litres (3 pints) with water. Add the sugar and allow it to start to dissolve, off the heat.

3   Cut the reserved oranges in half, and scrape all the seeds and pith into a bowl. Tie the pith and seeds up in a square of muslin. Finely shred the peel and the reserved ginger. Add the pith, seeds, peel, and ginger to the pan.

4   Bring the mixture to the boil, then simmer for 10 minutes. Add the ginger syrup and the preserved ginger. Continue to cook for a further 30 minutes, or until the marmalade has reached setting point. Pot into hot sterilized jars, seal, and label.

INGREDIENTS

1.25kg (2¾lb) Seville oranges

115g (4oz) fresh root ginger

1.5kg (3lb 3oz) unrefined granulated sugar

1 x 200g (7oz) jar preserved stem ginger in syrup, finely sliced

ENSURING SOFT PEEL

For marmalade-lovers, the delight is in the peel found in this traditional favourite. Do make sure that you are patient and always cook the fruit fully before you add the sugar. Otherwise the peel will toughen, and the finished preserve suffers as a result.

This takes a little effort, but the result is fabulous, sharp, and tangy – and perfect for morning toast and for those who prefer a lighter marmalade rather than the traditional chunky type.

Lemon shred marmalade

 TAKES 1¼ HOURS   MAKES 1.35KG (3LB)   KEEPS FOR UP TO 1 YEAR

1   Pare the peel from the lemons, as thinly as possible. The easiest method is to use a potato peeler. Shred the peel, and put in a large saucepan with 750ml (1¼ pints) water.

2   Bring to the boil, cover, and simmer for 30–40 minutes until the peel is very soft. Set aside to cool.

3   Meanwhile, roughly chop the peeled lemons and put the fruit, pips and all, in a preserving pan with 1 litre (1¾ pints) water. Bring to the boil, cover, and simmer for about 1 hour until the fruit is very soft.

4   Strain the liquid from the shredded peel into the pan, reserving the peel. Spoon the mixture into a jelly bag, and allow to drip overnight.

5   Measure the juice: you should have about 1 litre (1¾ pints). Put this in the cleaned preserving pan with the sugar. Heat gently until the sugar has dissolved, then increase the heat and cook at a full rolling boil for 5–10 minutes until the marmalade has reached setting point.

6   Skim off any scum, then stir in the reserved peel. Bring back to the boil and cook for 1 minute. Allow to stand for 5 minutes before potting into hot sterilized jars, sealing, and labelling.

INGREDIENTS

1kg (2¼lb) unwaxed lemons

1kg (2¼lb) white granulated sugar

This recipe comes from a friend's mother and is excellent for beginners. The fruit is minced using an old-fashioned mincer but it could be chopped by hand.

Easy everyday marmalade

 TAKES 1¼ HOURS  MAKES 2.5KG (5½LB) KEEPS FOR UP TO 1 YEAR

1 Put the fruit and 1.7 litres (3 pints) water in a preserving pan, cover, and simmer for 50–60 minutes until the fruit is very soft. Remove from the heat, lift out the fruit, and set aside to cool. Meanwhile, measure the liquid and make up to 1.4 litres (2½ pints) with water. Return to the pan, and stir in the sugar.

2 Halve the fruit and squeeze out the pips. Tie the pips in a square of muslin. Mince or chop the peel and flesh. Add to the pan with the bag of pips. Stir over a low heat until the sugar has dissolved.

3 Increase the heat and cook at a full rolling boil for 10–15 minutes until the marmalade has reached setting point. Remove and discard the pips, and pot the marmalade into hot sterilized jars, seal, and label.

INGREDIENTS

7 Seville oranges, scrubbed

2 sweet oranges, scrubbed

1 large lemon, scrubbed

1.35kg (3lb) white granulated sugar

This marmalade is usually called traditional or vintage as it has a rich caramel flavour, a chunky cut, and a good kick of whisky. No whisky in the house? Brandy works a treat!

Whisky marmalade

 TAKES 1½ HOURS  MAKES 2.7KG (9LB) KEEPS FOR UP TO 1 YEAR

1 Put the oranges and 2.25 litres (4 pints) water in a preserving pan, cover, and simmer for 50–60 minutes until the fruit is very soft. Remove from the heat, lift out the fruit, and cool. Measure the liquid and make up to 1.7 litres (3 pints) with water. Stir in the sugar.

2 Halve the oranges and scoop out the flesh and pips. Tie these in a square of muslin. Cut the peel coarsely. Add to the pan with the muslin bag. Stir over a low heat until the sugar has dissolved.

3 Increase the heat and cook at a full rolling boil for 10 minutes until the marmalade has reached setting point. Cool for 10 minutes. Stir in the whisky, pot into hot sterilized jars, seal, and label.

INGREDIENTS

1.5kg (3lb 3oz) Seville oranges, well washed

1.5kg (3lb 3oz) light muscovado sugar

4 tbsp whisky

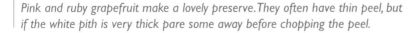

Pink and ruby grapefruit make a lovely preserve. They often have thin peel, but if the white pith is very thick pare some away before chopping the peel.

Pink grapefruit marmalade

🕐 TAKES 1½ HOURS   🍲 MAKES 1.6KG (3½LB)   🥫 KEEPS FOR UP TO 1 YEAR

1   Cut the fruit in half and carefully squeeze out all the juice, straining it into a large bowl. Reserve the pips. Store the juice and pips, covered, in the refrigerator until needed.

2   Using a sharp knife, cut the shells of the grapefruit and lemons into fine shreds. Put these in a large china or glass bowl, and cover with 1.5 litres (2¾ pints) water. Leave to soak for 24 hours.

3   Tie the reserved pips in a muslin bag. Put the fruit and water into a preserving pan with the reserved juice and the bag of pips. Bring to the boil, then simmer for 60 minutes until the peel is very soft. You must be able to cut it easily with a wooden spoon.

4   Stir in the sugar, and simmer over a low heat until this has dissolved. If any scum rises to the surface, skim it off as the mixture boils: you may need to do this several times. Now increase the heat and cook at a full rolling boil for 20–30 minutes, then test for a set.

5   When the marmalade has reached setting point, allow it to stand for 5 minutes, then pot into hot sterilized jars, seal, and label.

INGREDIENTS

3 pink- or red-fleshed grapefruit, scrubbed

2 large lemons, scrubbed

1.35kg (3lb) white granulated sugar

VARIATION
Yellow grapefruit work well here – do try to buy best-quality large fruit with no skin blemishes, to ensure you end up with a superior preserve.

Preserving citrus fruits

CHOOSING AND COOKING

Oranges, lemons, and limes – where would cooking be without these wonderful taste-enhancing fruits that add colour, flavour, and piquancy to such a variety of foods, both sweet and savoury? Add to this familiar trio other lesser-used citrus varieties such as grapefruit, mandarins, and kumquats, and you have an enticing range of basic ingredients with which to make jams, relishes, and other preserves.

What to look for

Choose ripe fruit without bruises or blemishes. Do not be misled by the colour of the skin: this is not always a good guide, as many citrus fruits are fully ripe when the skins are still quite green.

Softening the peel

When cooking citrus fruits, it is necessary to boil them in plenty of water before adding any sugar so that the peel is thoroughly cooked, or it may become tough and spoil the finished preserve. Both lemons and limes are especially difficult to cook, so allow plenty of time. Lemons are commonly used to add acid to low-acid preserves. Their juice is best used freshly squeezed. Most lemons yield 3 tablespoons (45ml/1½fl oz) or so of juice.

MAKE LIQUID PECTIN at home by boiling the shells left over once the juice has been used (see p15). The shells can be frozen until needed. Commercial pectin is made by boiling citrus skins in water to extract the pectin, then either bottling the resulting liquid or drying it to form a powder.

GRATE THE ZEST and add to marmalades. It may be grated coarsely for the classic chunky marmalade, or more finely for a more delicate preserve.

ORANGES AND LEMONS, the most familiar of all citrus fruits, are commonly sold with waxed skins to extend their shelf life and aid appearance. Before cooking, scrub the skins well to remove the wax coating. Alternatively, buy unwaxed citrus fruit.

RESERVE THE PITH AND PIPS when preparing the fruit; these contain most of the pectin. Secure them in a muslin bag, and boil along with the peel.

COOK CITRUS PEEL thoroughly until soft; if it is still tough, it may spoil the finished preserve.

No shreds at all this time, but a really tart, fragrant marmalade. Use ripe limes that have just begun to turn yellowish-brown. This marmalade reaches setting point quickly, so be prepared.

Lime jelly marmalade

🕐 TAKES 30 MINUTES 🍲 MAKES 1.35KG (3LB) 🥫 KEEPS FOR 6 MONTHS

1 Cut the limes in half and squeeze out the juice. Reserve the shells and the juice.

2 Finely chop the reserved shells in a food processor, or chop by hand. Put in a large preserving pan with 1 litre (1¾ pints) water. Bring the mixture to the boil, cover, and simmer for 20 minutes. Spoon, along with the reserved juice, into a jelly bag. Allow to drip overnight.

3 Pour the juice into the cleaned preserving pan, and add the sugar. Warm over a low heat, stirring, until the sugar has dissolved. Increase the heat and cook at a full rolling boil for about 1 minute, then test for a set. When the marmalade has reached setting point, pot into hot sterilized jars, seal, and label.

INGREDIENTS

750g (1lb 10oz) ripe limes, scrubbed

1kg (2¼lb) white granulated sugar

Kumquats have the odd distinction in the citrus family of having pith that is sweeter than the fruit inside. They make a rather sophisticated preserve, suited to the finest breakfast tables.

Kumquat marmalade

🕐 TAKES 40 MINUTES 🍲 MAKES 1.25KG (2¾LB) 🥫 KEEPS FOR 6 MONTHS

1 Cut the kumquats into fine slices. Remove the pips, catching the juice in a bowl. Tie the pips in a square of muslin, and put in a heavy preserving pan with the kumquats (and any juices), the lemon juice and zest, and 400ml (14fl oz) water. Cover the pan, and simmer for 25 minutes until the fruit is very tender.

2 Squeeze as much juice as possible out of the bag of pips, then discard the bag. Add the sugar, and stir over a low heat until the sugar has dissolved. Increase the heat and cook at a full rolling boil for 5 minutes, then test for a set.

3 When the marmalade has reached setting point, pot into hot sterilized jars, seal, and label.

INGREDIENTS

500g (1lb 2oz) kumquats

finely grated zest and freshly squeezed juice of 1 lemon

500g (1lb 2oz) white granulated sugar

Rather sweeter than most, clementine marmalade makes a lovely, rich breakfast treat. Though the fruit has very thin skin, it will still need some precooking to give a tender preserve.

Clementine marmalade

🕐 TAKES 40 MINUTES   🍲 MAKES 1.35KG (3LB)   🥫 KEEPS FOR 6 MONTHS

1   Discard any pips from the clementines, and whiz in a food processor until they are finely chopped, or chop by hand. Tip the fruit into a preserving pan, and add 1 litre (1¾ pints) water and the lemon juice. Bring to the boil and simmer for 7–10 minutes until the rind is soft.

2   Add the sugar, and stir until it has dissolved completely. Increase the heat and cook at a full rolling boil for 25 minutes, then test for a set.

3   When the marmalade has reached setting point, pot into hot sterilized jars, seal, and label.

INGREDIENTS

750g (1lb 10oz) clementines, washed and halved

freshly squeezed juice of 2 lemons

750g (1lb 10oz) white granulated sugar

Home-made lemon curd is amazing. I make mine with double cream, so this version is stored in the refrigerator, where it will keep, unopened, for 3–4 weeks.

Lemon curd

🕐 TAKES 25 MINUTES   🍲 MAKES 750G (1LB 10OZ)   🥫 KEEPS FOR 1 MONTH

1   Combine all the ingredients in a large, wide pan – I use a deep non-stick frying pan. Simmer the mixture over a low heat, stirring constantly with a wooden spoon, for 15–20 minutes until it begins to coat the back of the spoon. You must not let the mixture boil, so use a low heat and never leave the pan unattended.

2   When the curd is as thick as home-made mayonnaise, pot into hot sterilized jars and allow to cool for 5 minutes, before sealing and labelling. Allow the curd to cool completely, then store in the refrigerator until needed. Once opened, consume within a week.

INGREDIENTS

5 large eggs, beaten

200g (7oz) caster sugar

175ml (6fl oz) double cream

finely grated zest and freshly squeezed juice of 3 scrubbed or unwaxed lemons

Oranges and lemons are a more usual combination for this particular recipe, but limes add more fragrance than lemons. If the limes are very lacking in juice, add the juice of 1 lemon. This curd goes well on hot buttered crumpets or English muffins, or spoon it over meringues.

Orange and lime curd

 TAKES 40 MINUTES   MAKES 600G (1LB 5OZ)   KEEPS FOR 3 MONTHS

1 Using a very fine grater, grate the zest from the fruit, then squeeze out the juice.

2 Mix together the zests and juices in a wide heavy saucepan, and add the sugar, butter, and eggs. Place the pan over a low heat and simmer, whisking gently until the butter has dissolved.

3 Continue to cook the curd over a low heat, stirring constantly with a wooden spoon to ensure the curd does not stick to the pan. Watch it constantly, and remove from the heat as soon as it thickens. It should be the consistency of single cream. If you feel that the mixture is beginning to curdle, tip it into a large cold bowl, and whisk vigorously: this may save it. Alternatively, cook in a double boiler. This will take longer, but decreases the risk of curdling.

4 After removing the curd from the heat, stir again. If you feel the curd isn't quite thick enough, return to the heat and cook for a little longer, remembering that it will thicken further as it cools.

5 Once the mixture has achieved the desired consistency, pot into hot sterilized jars, seal, and label. Store in the refrigerator. Once opened, consume within a week.

INGREDIENTS

3 large oranges

2 large limes

200g (7oz) white granulated sugar

125g (4½oz) unsalted butter, diced

2 large eggs, beaten

A tangy pickle this, redolent of hot afternoons in India. I like its sharp, zesty flavour and slightly chewy texture. It works well with prawn curries, roasted chicken, Moroccan tagines, and hard cheeses such as Cheddar or manchego.

Lemon and apricot pickle

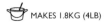 TAKES 35 MINUTES  MAKES 1.8KG (4LB)   KEEPS FOR UP TO 1 YEAR

1   Squeeze the juice from the lemons, and reserve. Using a food processor or knife, finely dice the lemon shells, onions, and apricots. If using a processor, do this in batches. Blend or process the garlic, ginger, and chillies to a paste. Alternatively, use a mortar and pestle.

2   Put all the ingredients, including the reserved lemon juice, in a large preserving pan, and warm over a medium heat. Once the sugar has dissolved, bring the mixture to the boil and simmer for 30 minutes until it thickens.

3   Pot into hot sterilized jars, cover with vinegar-proof seals, and label.

VARIATION
The mustard seeds make this pickle quite spicy, so for a milder taste replace them with crushed nigella seed. Nigella seed is also known variously as black onion seed, black caraway seed, or kalonji.

INGREDIENTS

500g (1lb 2oz) lemons

500g (1lb 2oz) large onions, chopped

250g (9oz) dried apricots

8–10 garlic cloves

50g (1¾oz) fresh root ginger

2–4 red chillies, deseeded if liked

400g (14oz) Demerara sugar

2 tbsp black mustard seeds

2 tbsp salt

500ml (16fl oz) white wine vinegar

Limoncello is a very sweet lemon liqueur that comes from the south of Italy near Sorrento. There, wonderful lemons with thick fragrant peel are steeped in alcohol, then sweetened with the addition of a sugar syrup. I have simplified the process in my recipe.

Limoncello vodka

🕐 NO COOKING   🍲 MAKES 1 LITRE (1¾ PINTS)   🥫 KEEPS FOR UP TO 1 YEAR

1   Begin by carefully peeling or grating all the yellow peel from the outside of the lemons. Take care not to include any of the white pith. I find a Microplane grater does this in the most efficient way.

2   Combine the vodka and lemon peel in a glass bowl, cover with cling film, and leave for 30 days in a cool, dark place.

3   Add the sugar and stir daily, covering the mixture again each time, until the sugar has completely dissolved.

4   Strain, discard the lemon peel, bottle the liqueur, seal, and label. Store in the freezer, and serve well chilled.

INGREDIENTS

8 unwaxed lemons

1 x 1 litre (1¾ pints) bottle full-strength vodka

250g (9oz) white granulated sugar

Sour oranges rather than sweet ones are the basis for this recipe, because it is the peel that's needed here. Rinse the oranges thoroughly and remove all the pith. Chopped before use, this condiment adds a lovely fragrance to Chinese cooking, game dishes, and tagines.

Salt-cured oranges

🕐 NO COOKING   🍲 MAKES 750G (1LB 10OZ)   🥫 KEEPS FOR 1 YEAR

1   Pack the orange quarters into glass jars, sprinkling with salt as you layer them. When the jars are full, add enough water to cover the fruit completely. Label the jars and secure the lids, then gently shake.

2   Look to see that there is still salt visible in each jar. If you can't see a layer of white salt, add more and keep on adding until the solution is saturated. Press the fruit under the liquid, and store in a cool, dark place, shaking the jars and topping up the salt from time to time. Store for about 6 weeks before using.

INGREDIENTS

4–6 Seville or other sour oranges, quartered

250g (9oz) coarse sea salt, plus extra as required

Jars of preserved lemons are a must-have ingredient these days. They look gorgeous and are simple to make. The down side? Well, you have to wait a few months before they're ready to use. Pack them into jars with glass lids to prevent the lids being corroded by salt. To use, scrape away the pith, finely chop the rind, and add to sauces, mashed potato, and tagines.

Preserved lemons

 NO COOKING   MAKES 1KG (2¼LB)   KEEPS FOR UP TO 2 YEARS

1 Scrub the lemons under hot water, and cut into quarters. Pack these into jars, adding a generous layer of salt between each layer. Push the lemons down well, then top up the jars with water. Put on the lids, then gently shake each jar. If all the salt dissolves, open the jar and add more.

2 Repeat the process each day for two weeks, gently shaking each jar and adding more salt if necessary. You must always be able to see a layer of salt sitting in the bottom of the jars. If you want the preserved lemons to look even prettier, tuck a couple of bay leaves and a chilli down the sides as you layer.

3 Store in a cool, dark place. Leave for 3 months before using.

INGREDIENTS

1kg (2¼lb) unwaxed lemons

250g (9oz) cooking salt, plus extra as required

bay leaves, to decorate (optional)

whole chillies, to decorate (optional)

USING THE PITH AND BRINE

I use the usually unwanted pith and salty liquid from preserved lemons to salt white fish such as cod, haddock, or pollock. Spread the pith and a few spoonfuls of liquid over the fish, leave to marinate for 1–2 hours, then rinse and cook.

Index

Acknowledgments

AUTHOR'S ACKNOWLEDGMENTS

Thank you to everyone involved with this lovely book. The pictures are beautiful and the editing a work of much patience and commitment, so my thanks go to Jean Cazals and Diana Craig, respectively. I was fortunate once again to have the unstinting support of my husband, Bob, and daughters, Jade and Amber, who proved committed critics and who washed up. Often. Dr Colin May, adviser to Certo Ltd, provided me with much learned correspondence on the subject of pectin, and I thank him for his patience as he helped me both to understand and to learn to love this useful substance. Good friends as ever have been supportive and forbearing, so thanks to Susan Flemming, Celia Kent, and Tim Etchells. Finally, my enduring thanks go to my mother, who taught me early of the many things in life that are worth preserving.

PUBLISHER'S ACKNOWLEDGMENTS

Dorling Kindersley would like to thank Valerie Barrett and Katie Rogers for recipe testing; and Hilary Bird for the index.

The publisher would also like to thank the following for their kind permission to reproduce their photographs:
(a-above; b-below/bottom; c-centre; f-far; l-left; r-right; t-top)
14 Kate Whitaker (r); 15 DK Library (l); 15 John Davis (r); 17 William Reavell (br); 20 DK Library (r); 21 Dave King (l); 21 Hugh Johnson (r)